The Dad Checklist

PRACTICAL SKILLS to TEACH YOUR CHILDREN

JEFF LEVINSON

STARTING NINE
A HISTORY COMPASS IMPRINT

Starting Nine, a History Compass Imprint
www.startingnine.com & www.historycompass.com

2nd edition © 2012 Jeff Levinson

Original edition © 2009 Jeff Levinson

ISBN: 978-1-932663-28-0

10 9 8 7 6 5 4 3 2 1
Printed in the United States of America.

— *To my family " from generation to generation,"*
Mom, Dad, W and M, and above all Lisa.

HOW TO CONTACT US:
We welcome your comments and ideas. Please feel free to share them
with us at thedadchecklist.com or go to startingnine.com.

Table of Contents

☐ Introduction 5

☐ **1.** The Outdoors Checklist 7

☐ **2.** The Sports Checklist 53

☐ **3.** The Tools, Repairs, & Woodworking Checklist 91

☐ **4.** Cars & Boats Checklist 113

☐ **5.** The Grilling & Home Cooking Checklist 131

☐ **6.** The Science & Technology Checklist 145

☐ **7.** The Culture Checklist 165

☐ **8.** The Fun Checklist 177

☐ **9.** The Family Checklist 191

✓ Introduction

The Dad Checklist gives fathers (and mothers) a quick reference of practical skills and information we want to pass along to our children. Dads have to remember a lot of things, like how to find the North Star, which cable goes where to jumpstart a car, how to remove splinters, the best way to teach a child to throw a baseball, and what to feed the children when Mom goes out.

It seems like there are so many things that we need to pass on to our children as they grow up. That is what I was thinking about one summer day standing in the backyard teaching my young sons how to throw and hit a baseball (they have been big into baseball for many seasons now). Ever since my first son was born, I had been thinking along these lines and had been jotting down ideas and notes. That day with my children, several thoughts crystallized. The more I thought about what I knew, the more I realized a few things:

1. What I didn't know was more than what I did know.

2. Thanks to my family, friends, and helpful people along the way, I had some great opportunities where I picked up the types of things that I wanted to pass along to my children and other children, like how to tie knots, paddle a canoe, patch drywall, build a wooden toolbox, explain why the sky is blue, and make chili.

3. I did not want to write a book about "surviving" being a father. Really what I was thinking about was what practical things I wanted to teach my children. Then, I thought about assembling information that all of us could use day to day. Putting that together was not easy (see #1 above). But as I drew on my experience, did my research, and began writing, the book evolved into *The Dad Checklist.* The checklist approach seemed natural since lots of us seem to be "hardwired" to use checklists, like with our home projects lists, woodworkers' cut lists, and the grocery lists we're handed on the way out the door.

Of course, I want to pass along good values to my children as my mother and father did, give my children opportunities, point them in the right direction, help them understand the difference between right and wrong, demonstrate honor and integrity, and help them to be happy. I'd like for them to understand the value of hard work, know that success comes from preparation and practice, tell the truth, respect others, and be kind, compassionate, and tolerant. That's something between my children and me. *The Dad Checklist* is about something else, something day to day, something a little easier than advising someone how to raise children. Plus, I admit up front that I don't have all the answers. But I have some ideas. So I assembled these ideas for the types of things we want to teach our children, from wilderness skills to science, from sports to culture, from grilling burgers to knowing that a full house beats a straight.

An added benefit to teaching your children some of the things in this book is the "wow" factor, as in "wow, Dad knows how to find south by his watch!" And, though this book is called the "Dad" Checklist, it is definitely for mothers, grandparents, uncles, aunts, cousins, guardians, and anyone else who can teach the skills to children.

In this book, I am trying to set out some guideposts or tools that might help us along the way. *The Dad Checklist* is the basic Swiss Army knife with a couple blades, a screwdriver, maybe those small tweezers. We should add our own tools to it, and at the same time hone the blades already there. I welcome your comments.

For now, let's roll up our sleeves, spit on our hands, and get to work.

—*Jeff Levinson*

The **Outdoors** *Checklist*

I went to the woods because I wished to live deliberately, to front only the essential facts of life, and see if I could not learn what it had to teach. . .

–Henry David Thoreau

As far as what dads should know, outdoor skills are near the top of the list. Dads are expected to know how to tie knots with ease, skip a rock with a flick of the wrist, forecast weather with a glance, remove splinters without pain, paddle a canoe without sweat, and navigate in the woods without getting lost.

Those outdoors skills that help you survive in the woods can be useful around the house. Knowing how to tie knots helps to secure the load on the car roof rack. Spending time in the backyard stargazing and pointing out constellations gives you a chance to share an invaluable experience with your children. Being outdoors with your children – in a park, in the woods, or around your neighborhood – gives you a chance to show your appreciation for nature.

When you are quiet, your child will take time to look at leaves lifting in the breeze, clouds scudding across the sky, a bird resting on a fence. Picking up a piece of trash on a trail will spark your child's understanding that we are stewards of the land, that we will leave the woods better than we found it. Enough preaching. Here are the practical things to teach about the outdoors.

✔ How to Tie Knots

Here are knots for many purposes, from tying a package to pitching a tent in a windy campsite. There are three key knots:

1. The basic square knot (plus its cousin, the sheet bend)
2. The bowline
3. Two half hitches (hitches are not technically knots)

☐ Square Knot

The square knot is the standard knot for tying two pieces of rope together that are the same thickness and is easy to tie.

A square knot is tied right over left, and then left over right. Pull tight. Be careful not to tie a "Granny Knot," which is right over left, right over left, because it is not very strong and will slip.

OUTDOORS NOTE: A "knot" ties the ends of two ropes. A "hitch" ties a rope to an object or itself. The end of the rope is called the "working end" or the "bitter end," which is what you hang on to. Knots reduce the strength of the line.

Sheet Bend Variation

A.

Cousin to a square knot, the sheet bend is used to tie two pieces of rope together when the ropes are different thicknesses. It is stronger and more reliable than the square knot.

A. Start by making a bend (shaped like a **J**) in the thicker rope. Thread the smaller diameter rope up through the bend and around behind both pieces of the thicker rope.

B. Bring the smaller diameter rope around to the front, then thread it under itself in the front part of the knot (so that when the knot is pulled tight, the smaller rope pulls down on itself). Tighten. This is what it should look like.

B.

Bowline

The bowline (pronounced "bo-lin") is used to tie a strong loop in the end of a rope, for rescues, harnesses, moorings, or whenever you need a loop that does not move. It can be used in place of a square knot to join two ropes securely together by their loops.

To tie a bowline, hold the rope near the end (known as the "free end"), and form a little loop a ways up from the end. How far "a ways" depends on how large you want your big loop and what you need it for. You'll be able to estimate loop size quickly after you've practiced this knot a few times.

A.

The little loop goes around so that the part of the rope leading to the free end is over, or in front, as you see in the first figure. Take the free end of the rope in your other hand, as you hold the little loop in the rope in place. Thread the free end up through the loop, around the back of the rope, and back down through the loop. Pull the knot tight. You now have a large loop in the end of the rope that will not easily slip.

The easy way to teach (and remember) how to tie this knot is that the rabbit comes up out of the hole, runs around the tree, and then goes back into his hole.

B.

A. Take the end of the rope and form a loop further up the rope (the top piece of the rope known as the "standing part," or the piece attached to an object, goes behind the loop).

B. While holding the loop in your left hand, hold the free end of the rope in your right hand. Thread the free end up through the loop. (Teach it as the free end of the rope being the rabbit, the loop being the hole, and the rope leading away as the tree. So the rabbit pops its head up out of the hole and jumps out.)

C.

C. And around the back of the long piece of rope that leads away. (The rabbit runs around the tree.)

D.

D. And back around and down through the loop. (The rabbit jumps back down into the hole.) Pull tight.

☐ Two Half Hitches

Two half hitches are easy to tie and useful for lashing stuff. They pull tightly against the object and hold well but should be tied off at the end.

A. Take the free end of the rope and loop it around the main part of the rope and back under the loop just formed.

B. Repeat the above to tie a second half hitch, so that the free end loops under the loop just formed. Tighten the loops by pulling the free end and sliding the loops down against the object you are securing.

You can get a lot of work done with the square knot, bowline, and two half hitches. Here are two bonuses the clove hitch, used tie a rope to a branch, pole, post, or pipe, and the tautline hitch, an adjustable hitch for tent lines.

(One way to untie knots: "Alexander finding himself unable to untie the Gordian Knot ... cut it asunder with his sword." —Plutarch's *Lives*)

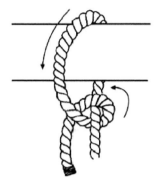

A.

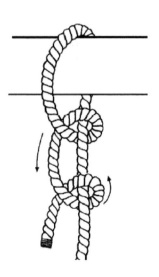

B.

☐ Clove Hitch

A. Take the free end of the rope and loop it around the pole (or branch, fence post, or pipe). (The standing end is on top of the first wrap around by the free end.)

B. When the free end comes back, pass it over the top of the rope leading away (standing end). Take the free end around the pole again just as you did with the first loop. But, this time, pass the free end on the inside of the loop you made.

C. The two loops sit next to each other. Pull both ends of the rope to tighten. Leave enough of the free end hanging so that it does not pull back through (or tie it off). (A variation, the "rolling hitch," has the free end wrap over the standing end, around the post twice, and loop under the top loop that it formed).

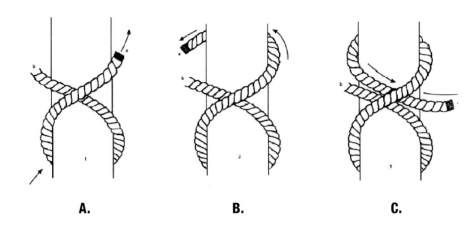

A.   **B.**   **C.**

☐ Tautline Hitch

A. One end of the rope will be secured to an object like a tent. Take the free end of the rope and loop it around the tent stake.

B. Make two turns around the standing line with the second turn closer to the stake.

C. Finish the hitch with a half hitch up the line, just past the two turns.

D. Tighten and slide the knot up or down to adjust the tension of the line.

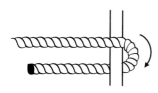

A.

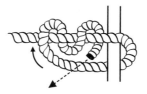

B.

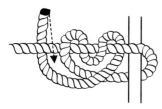

C.

D.

☑ Navigation

There may not be anyone around in the woods to ask directions (not that we would). Most of the time you'll want to stay on marked trails. Trails may be marked with paint marks or "blazes," signs, or sometimes painted marks on rocks. Other times you may go bushwhacking off the trail. How to get where you're going in the woods and how to get "unlost" are pretty useful skills.

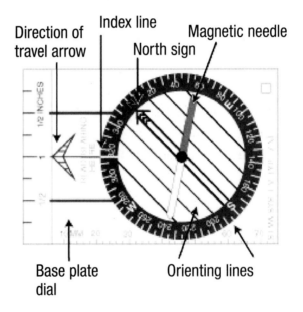

Direction of travel arrow

Index line

North sign

Magnetic needle

Base plate dial

Orienting lines

☐ Navigating with Map and Compass

Yes, there is GPS (global positioning system) technology, gadgets that use satellites to let you know within a few feet where you are. For those of us who don't have a GPS device or want to have that map and compass backup handy, here are some things to keep in mind. If you are on a trail and use your map, you will be able to follow along, using landmarks that you recognize, to know where you are, even without a compass.

Sometimes map reading can get you only so far, and you may need to use a compass. Here's how to figure out what direction you need to go and to follow the compass bearing.

Following a Bearing. Hold your compass out in front of you. Face the direction you want to go, and point the direction of travel arrow of your compass that direction. Twist the housing of the compass until the north (red) end of the needle lines up with the orienting arrow in the base of the housing. Your bearing – the direction to your destination – will be the degree number at the index line, that is, where the direction of travel arrow points.

> **OUTDOORS NOTE:** Keep the map in a ziploc bag to protect it from rain and river. It's a good idea for someone else in your group to have a set of maps, and everyone should carry a decent liquid-filled compass.

> **OUTDOORS NOTE:** The squiggly contour lines on topographic maps show heights. The closer the lines, the steeper the terrain.

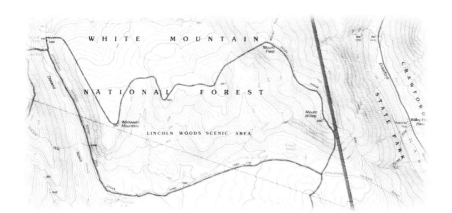

☐ Taking a Bearing from a Map

Say you wake up one morning on the trail and want to plan your route for the day. You know on the map where your campsite is located, just at the base of Cougar Mountain. And you know where you want to pitch your tent that evening, near Trout Lake a few miles away. Well, you can determine the direction on a map by doing the following:

1. Set the side edge of your compass on an imaginary line that connects where you are (the Cougar Mountain site) to where you want to go (the Trout Lake site).

2. Twist the compass housing until the meridian lines inscribed in the base of the housing line up with the map's north-south lines. Read the direction in degrees. That is your bearing.

3. To follow that bearing, hold your compass out in front of you and turn yourself (but not the compass housing) until the compass needle aligns with the orienting arrow in the housing. The direction of travel arrow on the baseplate will point to the Trout Lake site you want to reach.

You may also want to use your compass literally to "get your bearings." In other words, to orient your map, if you cannot do it by matching geographic features, adjust your compass for declination (see Outdoors Note on declination) according to the legend on your map. Set your compass down on your map, with the edge of the compass on the edge of your map and the direction of travel arrow pointing to the top of the map. Turn the

> **OUTDOORS NOTE:** If heavy forest or difficult trail make it so you can't hike exactly on your bearing, pick out points in between that are in the right direction, like a noticeable tree or boulder.
>
> Once you reach that particular landmark, pick out the next landmark farther on by taking another bearing. Follow successive landmarks until you reach your destination. You can check yourself by taking a back bearing to where you came from, 180 degrees opposite.

compass and map together until the compass needle is within the orienting arrow inscribed on the bottom of the housing.

How to Find South with a Watch

There is a "wow" way to use your watch as a rough compass. This can be used in an emergency, and it has a lot of value in demonstrating that dads know cool things.

Point the hour hand of your watch to the sun. Halfway between the hour hand and 12 is south!

Finding Your Way by the North Star

You can find north with the North Star (also known as Polaris). Locate the Big Dipper (see the Constellations section) and then the two stars at the end of the dipper's ladle. Those two stars make a line that points "up" to the North Star, which is part of the handle of the Little Dipper. You can also check whether you are facing east or west by which way the stars move – pick a star and see if it rises or sets. Rising stars show that you are facing east. Setting stars show you are facing west.

OUTDOORS NOTE: A critical thing to remember about compasses is that the needle does not actually point straight north. The compass points to "magnetic north," which may not align with "true north" except by coincidence. This is "declination." Magnetic north is related to the earth's magnetic field, shifts over time, and varies depending on where you are. So, when you are using a map, there will be a legend telling you what the difference is in degrees between magnetic north and true north, the declination.

Take the declination into account when using map and compass together (not necessary if you are just following a bearing). If your compass does not have an adjustable declination arrow, you have to make the adjustments manually.

☐ What to Do if You Get Lost

Keep your cool. Stop. Check your map. Try to figure out when and where you (or the lost person) were last. The usual rule is to stay where you are, but you have to use good judgment. If you stay, don't panic, and make sure that rescuers can find you. (You should leave a trip plan with someone and instructions on what to do if you do not return by a certain time.) If you need to get out, following a stream downhill will often lead to civilization, but sometimes not so out West where some streams lead to inaccessible canyons.

While it is unlikely to happen, you should teach your children that if they get lost in the woods to stop and stay right where they are. Teach younger children to "hug a tree," to find one tree right where they are and stay with it. Teach them to blow their whistle from time to time. Tell your children that you will find them. Let them know that if you get separated, nothing bad will happen to them, no animals will hurt them, and that you will find them no matter what. They should have their own water, but teach them to sip the water when they are thirsty, not to drink it all up at once. As a parent, do not panic. Call out and use your whistle. Check the immediate area to see if the child has wandered off close by. If not, send someone for help.

OUTDOORS NOTE: You may want to give each child his or her own "emergency kit" in case they get lost. You can have this as part of their backpacks, or, if they are not carrying a full pack, part of their day packs or even as hip packs. Let them help choose what goes in it, including a (small) special toy or stuffed animal.

They should also have a mylar blanket, bandanna, small flashlight or lightstick, whistle, water bottle, snack bar, and extra bandaids. Go over what the kit is for and what to do if someone gets lost.

✓ First Aid

As we used to say in Boy Scout Troop 25 in Memphis, "Be Prepared." A basic first aid kit should be one of the first things you pack for your trip. If your child has specific medical requirements, bring what you need, like a bee sting kit, asthma inhaler, or other medicines. Be careful about hypothermia, a real problem for children since they are smaller than we are and get cold more quickly. At the same time, in hot weather, children can become dehydrated quickly, so make sure that they are drinking enough water. (One way to know if you're drinking enough water- your urine is clear or light yellow. If it is dark yellow, you need more water). A Red Cross CPR and First Aid course will help you understand what to do in an emergency, and there is no substitute for your common sense. If you're in the wilderness, figure out emergency take out places in advance.

☐ First Aid Kit

Kids are fascinated by first aid kits, and band aids are always in demand. Here are some key items, which you should pack in a durable, waterproof container:

- ☐ Assorted bandaids.
- ☐ Wound cleanser (soap and water, hydrogen peroxide, or commercially available preparations).
- ☐ Antiseptic and/or alcohol wipes.
- ☐ Roll of adhesive tape.
- ☐ Small scissors (if not on your knife or multi-purpose tool) for cutting adhesive tape, gauze, and moleskin.

- [ ] Needle or safety pin and tweezers for removing splinters.
- [ ] Thermometer in hard case.
- [ ] Moleskin and molefoam for blisters.
- [ ] Antibacterial ointment like Neosporin.
- [ ] Small Vaseline.
- [ ] Assorted gauze pads.
- [ ] Aspirin and/or ibuprofen and children's pain reliever.
- [ ] Antacid.
- [ ] Antihistamine (Benadryl tablets).
- [ ] Bee sting kit, if someone is allergic.
- [ ] Anti-diarrhea medicine (Imodium).
- [ ] Anti-itch cream (hydrocortisone, Benadryl).
- [ ] Personal medication. Make sure you check before you go.
- [ ] Ace bandage.
- [ ] Bandannas (lots). Can be used to cover wounds, make slings, and tie splints. (They also make handy potholders, head coverings, towels, and tiedowns.)

Medicine and Other First Aid We Need to Remember:

- [ ] _____
- [ ] _____
- [ ] _____
- [ ] _____
- [ ] _____

[ ] Splinter Removal Procedure

The Splinter Removal Procedure is a critical dad skill, on the trail or around the house. If you are removing a splinter from a young child, the most important part is distraction. Keep them talking about other things, anything but what you are doing to that finger. If the splinter is big enough and still sticking out of the skin, you can probably remove it with tweezers. Clean the tweezers with an alcohol wipe, extract the splinter, clean the wound, apply antibacterial cream, and cover with a band aid.

If the splinter is too small or is under the skin, lay out your operating equipment: needle or safety pin, tweezers, alcohol wipes, antibacterial cream, and bandaid. Take the needle or safety pin and sterilize the point by wiping it with an alcohol wipe (in the old days, fathers would do this by holding the point in a lighter flame). Clean the area on and around the splinter with alcohol. Get some distracting conversation going about what kind of snacks you packed.

Once your child's attention is not entirely focused on the splinter and the needle, you are ready to begin the procedure. Hold the finger in one hand and squeeze gently so that the skin with the splinter stands out a little. Then, very gently, work the needle to try to scrape the splinter out. The angle of the needle depends on where the splinter is lodged. If a little bit of splinter protrudes from the skin, you can sometimes catch hold of it with the end of the needle and back it out the way it got in. If it is too deep, you will have to gently scrape away the top layer of skin until you can scrape out the splinter. Keep the needle at a low angle to scrape and pull the splinter without pricking or jabbing the finger.

> **REALITY CHECK:** By the way, no matter what distraction method you employ, your child will still fidget, so see what you can do, take a break if you need to, and restart the procedure after everyone has calmed down.

☐ Dealing with Blisters

Avoid blisters. It helps to have good hiking boots that have been broken in before the big hike, plus good socks. There are good lightweight boots that fit pretty comfortably out of the box, but they should still be broken in or tested for fit before the trip. For major hiking, use synthetic liner socks with wool or wool blend outer socks or just one layer wearing something like smartwool socks. Cotton socks get wet from sweat and bunch up. They can be really uncomfortable if you are on a long hike and can accelerate blistering.

If you feel a "hot spot," stop hiking and deal with it right then. Don't be a hero and charge on. Tell your children to tell you any time their feet hurt (though you may get more than you bargained for in response). Ask everyone you are hiking with, especially children, if their feet are getting rubbed too much or if their feet feel "hot" anywhere. Even if they don't say anything, if they are fairly young and you are on a long hike, you might want to inspect their feet occasionally. Blisters can make every step agony, and not only do you not want your child to suffer, but you also do not want to end up carrying a heavy little body down the trail.

If the spot is just red, you can cover it with a band aid and strip of adhesive tape, Spenco Second Skin, or small square of moleskin. If a blister has already formed, you will need to get out the moleskin (or thicker molefoam) and scissors. Medical "experts" sometimes caution not to pop the blister. (I have my own views on this. If I were going to do it, I would make sure that the area was cleaned with an alcohol wipe and that the needle was sterilized before I popped the blister and then would use antibacterial cream and a band aid.) To protect the blister area, build up moleskin around the blister like a doughnut by cutting the center out of the piece of moleskin so that the rest of the moleskin surrounds the blister. This takes the pressure off the blister. Cover the "doughnut hole" with a band aid or piece of adhesive tape to protect the skin under it. Some hikers use duct tape for hot spots and blisters.

☑ Canoeing

Dads can demonstrate real dad skills when out in a canoe. To look like experienced backwoodsmen, bow and stern paddlers paddle on opposite sides. You don't need to paddle on the same side, because you can make the canoe travel in a straight line using the right stroke. Also, unless you are in rapids or rough water where you want to keep the canoe's center of gravity low, it is acceptable to sit on the seats, rather than kneel, in the canoe. The best places to canoe are anywhere near your home that you can borrow or rent a canoe and paddle along with your children, gauged at everyone's age, experience, and swimming ability. One great place is the Boundary Waters Canoe Area in Minnesota, but there likely will be somewhere near you that you will enjoy.

☐ Three Basic Canoeing Strokes

1. Straight paddle. For the basic power stroke, hold your paddle at the throat, where the shaft meets the blade, and at the grip at top. Reach the blade ahead, dip the blade fully in the water ahead of you, and pull back strongly. The blade should go deep enough into the water so that your hand at the paddle's throat gets wet.

Pull through and really move some water. You want the blade
to move most of the water while it is mostly vertical in the water
(the last part of the stroke, where you are pulling the blade up out
of the water lifts water up but does not move you forward).

Twist at the waist as you paddle through and focus on using your
stronger back, chest, and core muscles instead of just your arm
muscles. At the end of your stroke, "feather" the blade, meaning
twist it so that the long edge of it cuts through the wind as you
pivot the blade forward. Feathering reduces wind resistance.
(You can reverse the straight paddle stroke to move the canoe
backward.)

REALITY CHECK: For children starting out, a very short paddle
and sitting on your lap for a few minutes on a calm lake or slow
river might be the way to introduce them to canoeing.

2. J-stroke. The laws of canoe physics state that if the bow and
stern paddlers are both straight paddling on opposite sides,
the canoe will still turn opposite the side the stern paddler is
paddling on. If the stern person is paddling on the right side, the
canoe will veer to the left, or opposite side.

One way to control the natural turn of the canoe is to have the
paddlers switch sides, but then you end up zigzagging across the
lake plus you waste energy switching sides so often. A skillful and
efficient way to keep the canoeing moving straight is for the stern
paddler to use a **J** shaped stroke, creatively called a "**J** stroke."

For the **J** stroke in the stern, begin your stroke like a straight paddle. As the blade nears the end of the pull cycle, twist your hands in and over toward the front of the canoe, counterclockwise if paddling on the right side and clockwise if paddling on the left. That is, the thumb of your top hand will turn down and point toward the water. Near the end of the stroke, your blade should be angled slightly in the water and acts like a rudder, correcting the turn you would have made if you were just straight paddling. Hold the blade out at that angle (about 20–30 degrees) for an instant before lifting the blade out of the water and feathering it as you reach forward for your next stroke. Canoeing is a team effort, so the stern person should not leave his blade in the water too long and use it as a rudder without contributing power to the canoe's forward motion. It is ok to lever the paddle off the gunwale (edge) but not to bang the gunwale if you can help it.

One other thing: some paddlers are moving from using the **J**-stroke to switching sides often to keep the canoe straight, much as canoe racers do. If you are on a long river or lake trip, try both to see which you prefer.

3. Sweep. To turn the canoe, the stern paddler can make a sweep, a **C**-shaped stroke in the water. Reach forward and put the blade in the water as you would a straight or **J**-stroke, but instead of pulling straight back, pull around in a backward **C**. The canoe will turn to the side opposite the one you're paddling on. A "reverse sweep" is the opposite. Put the blade in behind you, and "sweep" it in a semicircle or reverse **C** out toward the front. This stroke will turn the canoe in the direction of the side the stern

OUTDOORS NOTE: To grip the paddle, your top hand should grasp around the top of the paddle grip. Your hand will be over the top, not around it like a bat. The bottom hand grips around the throat of the paddle, in an overhand grip, all the way down so that your hand just touches the top part of the blade.

The pear grip is comfortable for longer paddle trips, while the **T** grip is often used more for whitewater canoeing. An oval shaft is more comfortable compared to a round shaft. A straight shaft is more common for all around canoeing, but flatwater paddlers will pick a bent shaft paddle for long trips. I have a strong aesthetic preference for traditional wood paddles. If you own a wood paddle, you can paint the blade! Also, on canoe trips you will want to carry a spare paddle.

person is paddling on. The sweeps are not power strokes, but they will turn you faster than a **J** or series of straight strokes.

You can maneuver a canoe pretty much wherever you need to, especially in open water, if you master the straight paddle, **J**-stroke, and sweep.

☐ Paddling Safety

Know how to swim. Wear life jackets. If you shoot rapids, know what you are doing, scout them, and be humble. If they look too rough or you do not yet have the experience, portage (carry) the canoe around the rapids. Those portages are there for a reason. Learn from someone experienced what to do if your canoe swamps.

REALITY CHECK. For younger children, short canoe trips help get them used to canoeing and prepared for longer journeys. If you have a nearby canoe rental place or have a canoe you can borrow and take on a calm lake or river, those are your best bets. An hour or so the first few times out (with good snacks) is about all that younger children can take. They are sitting still in the bottom of a boat without games or toys so it's up to you to provide the entertainment.

☐ Portaging

One person portaging is an art. The quick way to explain how to do it is to pull the canoe out of the water, stand next to the canoe, face the direction you plan to go (both you and the canoe should be facing forward down the trail), bend over so that your far hand

---

OUTDOORS NOTE: The stern paddler is responsible for keeping the canoe on course (except in rapids, in which case both paddlers have to help guide the canoe). On open water, pick a point in the distance where you want to go, like a tall tree across a lake. Aim and paddle.

If the wind is pushing you to the side, you'll want to angle into the wind so that your true course is in the direction you want to go. If the wind is hitting you broadside, like across a large lake, be careful and angle into it to avoid being swamped. In rapids, the stern paddler sets the initial course line, but the bow paddler is responsible for calling out rocks and helping avoid them.

reaches over and grips the far side of the middle thwart (the bar that goes across the canoe that has the portaging yoke or cutout place for your neck) near the far gunwale (edge) and the near hand grips the thwart close to the near gunwale. Pull the canoe up onto your thigh, near hand holding it in tight and far hand reaching over to the far side of the thwart. Rock the canoe that is resting on your thigh, and on three flip it up over your head and settle it down on your shoulders with the yoke pads or thwart resting on your shoulders. The trick is to have the canoe flow smoothly up, over, and down, and not try to muscle it up. Then, extend one or both arms to hold the bow steady and straight, and off you go down the portage, swatting mosquitoes along the way.

☑ Weather

☐ Predicting the Weather

Here are three sayings that originated in old sailing ship days to help predict the weather.

1. "Red sky at night, sailors delight. Red sky at morning, sailors take warning." I heard this saying first from my father. If you see a red sky at night, you should have good weather the next day. If you see red sky in the morning, watch for a storm.

2. "When the dew is on the grass, rain will never come to pass. When grass is dry at morning light, look for rain before the night."

> **OUTDOORS NOTE:** To tell how far away a storm is, count from the time you see the lightning flash until you hear the thunder. Every five seconds equals one mile. If the time between lightning and thunder decreases each time you count it, the storm is moving closer.

3. "A ring around the moon is a sure sign of rain." High clouds signaling bad weather make a halo around the moon. You can also predict rain when pine cones are closed up. There are the obvious signs: if you see puffy white cumulus clouds begin to build up, keep a close eye on the sky. If the clouds get higher or grayer or form anvil heads, a bad storm is coming. If you hear thunder or see lightning, get away from single trees, shallow caves, and exposed areas like ridges. Obviously get off or out of the water.

☐ Cloud Recognition

What you should know about clouds is clustered around where they appear in the sky; what you should look for is how they develop.

High Clouds: High clouds like the wispy *cirrus* clouds and puffy white *cirrocumulus* mean fair weather. The exception to the high clouds, fair weather rule of thumb are the sheets of *cirrostratus* clouds that indicate an advancing cold front and rain or snow. The saying, "A ring around the moon is a sure sign of rain," refers to what happens when sheets of cirrostratus cover the sky.

Cirrus

Cirrocumulus

Cirrostratus

(Cloud photos from Virtualskies/NASA)

Middle Clouds: Gray middle level clouds like *altostratus* that cover the sky and puffy *altocumulus* usually mean rain, thunderstorms, or snow.

Altostratus

Altocumulus

Low Clouds: Low clouds usually mean some kind of rain, as with the long gray *stratus* clouds (drizzle), low gray *stratocumulus* (light drizzle), and dark gray *nimbostratus*. Dark gray nimbostratus clouds are what you would think of if you were thinking about rain.

Stratus

Stratocumulus

Nimbostratus

Low to High Clouds: Two types of clouds start low and go up: puffy fair weather *cumulus* and easily recognizable severe storm *cumulonimbus*, which harbors severe lightning.

Cumulus

Cumulonimbus

☐ Wind Chart

The Beaufort scale (named after English Rear Admiral Sir Francis Beaufort who created it in 1805) is a quick way to estimate wind speed though, really, if it is cold and windy, it's cold and windy.
(1 knot = 1.15 mph)

Force	Wind (Knots)	Description	Wind Effects On Water	Wind Effects On Land
0	Less than 1	Calm	Sea surface smooth and mirror-like	Calm, smoke rises vertically
1	1–3	Light Air	Ripples	Smoke drift indicates wind
2	4–6	Light Breeze	Small wavelets, crests glassy	Wind felt on face, leaves rustle, weather vanes move
3	7–10	Gentle Breeze	Large wavelets, crests begin to break, scattered whitecaps	Leaves and small twigs constantly moving, light flags extended
4	11–16	Moderate Breeze	Small waves 1–4 ft. becoming longer, numerous whitecaps	Dust, leaves, and loose paper lifted, small tree branches move
5	17–21	Fresh Breeze	Moderate waves 4–8 ft. taking longer form, many whitecaps, some spray	Small trees in leaf begin to sway
6	22–27	Strong Breeze	Larger waves 8–13 ft., whitecaps common, more spray	Larger tree branches moving, whistling in wires

Force	Wind (Knots)	Description	Wind Effects On Water	Wind Effects On Land
7	28–33	Near Gale	Sea heaps up, waves 13–20 ft., white foam streaks off breakers	Whole trees moving, resistance felt walking against wind
8	34–40	Gale	Moderately high (13–20 ft.) waves of greater length, foam blown in streaks	Whole trees in motion, resistance felt walking against wind
9	41–47	Strong Gale	High waves (20 ft.), sea begins to roll, dense streaks of foam, spray may reduce visibility	Slight structural damage occurs, slate blows off roofs
10	48–55	Storm	Very high waves (20–30 ft.) with overhanging crests, sea white with densely blown foam, heavy rolling, lowered visibility	Seldom experienced on land, trees broken or uprooted, considerable structural damage
11	56–63	Violent Storm	Exceptionally high (30–45 ft.) waves, foam patches cover sea, visibility more reduced	
12	64+	Hurricane	Air filled with foam, waves over 45 ft., sea completely white with driving spray, visibility greatly reduced	

☑ Constellations

Picture this. You're standing outside, your child close by your side, looking up into the night sky. You raise your finger and point at a distant star (aren't they all distant?), and say:

A. "We were just laughing about the apparent retrograde motion of that magnitude four red dwarf the other day down at the observatory."

B. "Do you see those stars that look like a big ladle?"

C. "Those are stars."

If you selected "A", please write to give me some tips. If you want to be able to point to a few beautiful constellations, keep reading. If you like answer "C", hum "Twinkle Twinkle" when you say it.

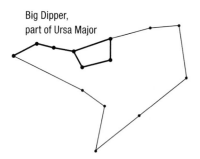

Big Dipper,
part of Ursa Major

☐ Big Dipper

Look up in the night sky to find the easily-recognizable Big Dipper, part of the constellation known as Ursa Major (Big Bear), which looks like this.

Little Dipper

You can find the Little Dipper (Ursa Minor or Little Bear) by tracing the line from the two stars at the end of the Big Dipper's ladle part, up to the end of the Little Dipper. You will see the North Star, which marks the end of the Little Dipper's handle and North. If you follow it down, you can see the handle and the ladle part of the dipper. The Little Dipper looks like this.

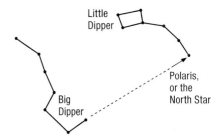

Draco

Once you've found the Big Dipper and Little Dipper, it's easy to find Draco the Dragon, whose tail winds between the Big and Little Dippers. Draco has a diamond-shaped head and long tail. Draco looks like this.

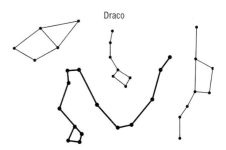

Here are three more easy-to-spot constellations:

Cassiopeia

Cassiopeia looks like a flattened "**M**," like this.

☐ Orion

Orion the Hunter is clear in winter. You can pick out Orion's body, as well as his belt with sword hanging off of it. If you follow Orion's belt to the east, you will find Canis Major with bright Sirius, the Dog Star. Orion looks like this.

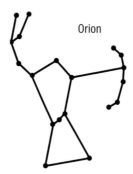

Orion

☐ Scorpius

You can spot Scorpius low in the summer sky. Scorpius looks like this.

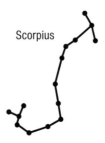

Scorpius

☑ Moons by Month

Month	Moon Type
January	Wolf Moon, Old Moon
February	Snow Moon, Hunger Moon
March	Maple Sugar Moon, Sap Moon, Worm Moon, Crow Moon
April	Frog Moon, Pink Moon, Planter's Moon, Grass Moon
May	Flower Moon, Budding Moon, Milk Moon
June	Strawberry Moon, Rose Moon
July	Blood Moon, Buck Moon, Thunder Moon
August	Green Corn Moon, Sturgeon Moon, Red Moon
September	Harvest Moon
October	Hunter's Moon, Falling Leaves Moon
November	Beaver Moon, Frost Moon
December	Cold Moon

OUTDOORS NOTE: "Blue Moon" means the second full moon in one month.

☑ How to Skip Rocks

It's a scene from a movie – father and child walking along the beach skipping rocks together looking out over the vast sea. The old proverb goes that when you teach your son, you teach your son's son and so on to the end of generations. Generations of fathers and daughters and sons have skipped rocks together at the sea, as my father taught me and as I taught my sons. There are three simple steps to keeping your part of the chain: The Search, The Grip, The Skip.

1. The Search. Find a smooth, flat, silver dollar sized or slightly larger rock about half an inch thick.

2. The Grip. Hold the rock flat, parallel to the water, with your index finger curved around the edge. You will probably bend down a little to get closer to water level.

3. The Skip. Whip the rock sidearm and flat, out across the water. All that's left is to count the skips across the water and revel together in the moment.

☑ How to Build Fires

☐ Outdoors

Like most things in life, preparation is the key. Before you light the fire, build it right and collect enough wood to keep it going. If it's windy build your file in a sheltered place, but not too close to anything that you don't want to catch. (If you are camping, make sure that fires are allowed and build them only in permitted areas. Otherwise, take a cooking stove and fuel.)

Start with tinder. This is small, easily lighted material like birch bark in northern climates (off the ground, not peeled from the tree), small twigs, and shavings from a piece of dry wood. Place the tinder in the center of your fire. Around it, build up some thin pieces of kindling in the form of a teepee. Do not crowd the pieces, as there should be space for air to circulate. You should be able to light the tinder from down low with one match (the one match fire being the sign of a real wilderness man). Once the kindling has caught, feed larger pieces of wood one by one to get the fire roaring.

When you are done, make sure that the fire is out. There could be embers buried in there that are still burning so douse it thoroughly and stir to make sure it is out.

REALITY CHECK: Children love to help build fires. In the wilderness, they can help. Have them help clear out the fire site/pit area. Send them to collect kindling. Usually they will keep in view and search within a 10 foot radius of the firepit. Marvel at the rotted, fungal, decayed three inch sticks they bring in. The better part is to let them place their sticks on the unlit fire. They will be proud of helping out. Once they get a little older, they should be able to add sticks to a burning fire, approaching from low on the side and placing the fuel on the burning fire while learning not to throw the sticks just anywhere.

☐ **Indoors**

The fire in the indoor fireplace is built roughly the same way, though you do have the extra step of making sure that the chimney flue is open. Ball up several single sheets of newspaper and shove them under the metal grate. On the grate itself, put a large log in back and a smaller log in front, with space in between the two. In the space in between, put three or four pieces of balled up newspaper. Above that, spanning the two logs, lay some kindling, thin pieces of wood about six inches long. The pieces of kindling do not need to touch each other since air circulation is important. Above the pieces of kindling, cross hatch some thicker pieces of wood. Light the newspaper from the bottom. Once the fire is going, you can put a third log across the other two base logs, at an angle, and it should burn nicely.

A journey of a thousand miles begins with a single step. . .

–Lao Tze

☑ Camping

Safety, Comfort, and Fun

Safety Tips: Safety is your first priority.

☐ Use good judgment.

☐ You do not have to be the toughest person out there. The strong leader is the one who makes it ok not to take unnecessary risks. You can have a good, tough hike or canoe trip within everyone's comfort zone even while pushing those zones.

☐ Be prepared for the trail. Leave your schedule with someone. Read guidebooks. Check with the rangers for recent trail info. Understand what you may meet on the trail in the way of weather, bugs, animals, rough terrain, and water sources.

☐ When you are leading the trip, make sure everyone is safe and comfortable. For the basics, take Red Cross CPR and First Aid courses. Carry a first aid kit and map and compass and know how to use them. Carry appropriate clothing and raingear (because one rule of camping that we had at my college's freshman outdoor program is "It will rain"). Treat your drinking water. On the trail, prevent blisters, make sure that everyone is drinking enough water, make sure that your children's clothes are dry and sleeping bags warm (you will get cold and wet; be prepared), and consider what might make your children scared and talk to them about it.

☐ Have fun. Take pictures, and, if your children are old enough, have them keep a trip journal or write about their experience afterward.

Before You Go

☐ Get required permits.

☐ Select your route, with entry and exit points, and let someone else know about it and what your schedule is. Be in shape for the trail you've chosen. Know what to expect and prepare for the unexpected.

Our Camping Trips

Date   Where

_____

_____

_____

_____

_____

Where We'd Like to Go Next

☐ _____

☐ _____

☐ _____

☐ _____

☐ _____

☐ Prepare your equipment. Waterproof your boots, set up and inspect your tent, test your canoe and backpack and stove, sharpen your knife, pack up.

☐ Doublecheck to make sure that you have your critical gear, including medicines.

While You're Out There

☐ Leave the wilderness better than you found it.

☐ Pack it in, pack it out – take all your trash with you. Make a last check of your campsite or snack spot on the trail for any trash.

☐ To minimize damage to the woods, hike on the trail and camp at designated sites, away from rivers, lakes, and trails. Do not tear up trees, strip off bark, or pull down limbs. Do not move stuff around to design your site. Take the woods as they come.

☐ Do not pollute also means no noise pollution. Leave electronic gear, radios, and games at home. If you have to bring a cell phone for calling a ride at the end of trip, turn it off while you're out on the trail. You can leave your watch in the bottom of your pack, too. There's not really much call for it since you can eat when you're hungry, rest when you're tired.

☐ Be courteous on the trail. Let faster hikers go through. Keep voices down and be respectful of where you are. With children,

Wilderness is a resource that can shrink but not grow.

– Aldo Leopold

take breaks but also encourage them to push themselves a bit.

☐ Check with the rangers before you wander in the woods to get the latest info on trail conditions and any animals. Learn good practices to avoid attracting animals to you and your food (no food in the tent) and to protect yourself if you're in bear country, like using bear bags.

REALITY CHECK: Back when I used to lead one and two week canoeing and backpacking trips, I can assure you that I did not think highly of people who would go "car camping." Times change. I am now one of the car campers. There's probably a lesson in humility there. So, what happens is this. You are a rugged outdoorsman, and you and your friends enjoy challenging trails up rugged mountains. Then, you have a child or two. You are pretty sure that your children are too heavy to carry very far on a trail and probably wouldn't enjoy a long hike with less than extravagant amounts of snacks.

If you still want to camp out, then, you might have to adjust your sights and think about car camping just to get the kids out there and used to sleeping in a tent without a night light. Before you go, set up the tent in the backyard so that they can crawl around inside it. Let them know what to expect. Find a place that you can drive to. On our first trip, we just did a short overnight. It was enough to cook outdoors over a stove, hike a little both days, and sleep in a tent in sleeping bags. That was a memorable and successful trip.

OUTDOORS NOTE: You can tell how long until sunset without a watch – hold your hand up sideways to the horizon so that your fingers span the space between the horizon and the sun. Sunset will be in 15 minutes per finger.

SELECTING A KNIFE: Since you will use your knife daily on the trail and rely on it for everything from preparing dinner to cutting rope to making shavings for a fire, it should be of good quality, durable, and sharp. I like the utility of the (moderate sized) Swiss Army knife (the scissors are useful), but I prefer to carry in addition a single blade knife like a Buck sheath knife for cooking and cutting. Some people really like the multipurpose tools (the pliers can be used for lifting pots off the stove), though there is a tradeoff in weight. Take care of your knife and keep it sharp. A dull blade makes you put more pressure on the blade and heightens the risk it will slip.

Gear – A Checklist

☐ Map and compass. If you know how to use GPS, go ahead, but you just might want to keep a compass as a backup.

☐ Permits and licenses, ID, $.

☐ First Aid kit.

☐ Pen, pencils, and paper.

☐ Book (plus deck of cards, cribbage board).

☐ Whistle.

☐ Matches and lighter. Waterproof matches are reliable.

☐ Knife.

☐ Bandannas.

☐ Water bottles. Many people like the Nalgene bottles. Make sure that you have enough water bottles for each person and extra for emergencies.

☐ Water purification or filter. Neccessary for wilderness areas or anywhere you are not sure of the water supply. Before you go, check with the local outfitters or outdoors store for the best way to clean the water for the area you'll be traveling in. Be sure that your children know which water is safe to drink.

☐ Raingear. I recommend rain pants and rain jacket. Ponchos do not work well and get caught on branches and drag on the ground.

☐ Flashlight or headlamp with new batteries.

☐ Lightweight binoculars (optional).

☐ Camera.

☐ Glasses and sunglasses. Children, too, should have sunglasses. It makes no sense to me when I see parents wearing sunglasses on a bright day, and the children have no eye protection.

☐ Sunscreen. My wife has educated me on this.

☐ Chapstick.

☐ Bug spray.

☐ Hat or cap.

☐ TP (toilet paper) is high on the list of key items.

☐ Toiletries (toothbrush, toothpaste, biodegradable soap, personal meds, personal hygiene products; no razor because not only is shaving not required, but the rugged look is part of the experience).

Other Gear We
Need to Remember

☐ _____

☐ _____

☐ _____

☐ _____

☐ _____

☐ _____

☐ _____

☐ Repair kit. Sewing kit with (large) needles, thread, safety pins, small coil of wire, and fishing line for stronger repair. Multi-use duct tape for patching tents, boots, water bottles, canoes (along with liquid aluminum for canoes or some epoxies that harden like steel). Some ripstop nylon patches and tape-on velcro for tents and raingear. Spare backpack buckle. Extra cord. Extra lighter. Phone change or phone card (if you have a cell phone, it won't likely work in most wilderness areas though it might be useful in emergencies if you get close to a road. Remember to keep it off during the trip though). Hose clamp and cotter pins for your pack.

☐ Tent (already seam sealed) with poles, stakes, ground cloth, and rain fly. Lightweight tarp, as needed. Freestanding dome tents come in many shapes and provide great protection from wind and rain. Most come with a rainfly that covers the tent and shock-corded aluminum or fiberglass poles. They're easy to set up and come in all sizes.

☐ Light cord (for clotheslines, tying gear), about 50 feet of it.

☐ Bear bag and rope (if needed).

☐ Mylar (space blanket) emergency blanket (smaller than a deck of cards).

☐ Food. You can eat well on the trail. Make sure you bring enough food, since you burn more calories on the trail. You have to carry just about everything you plan to eat (not a problem if you are car camping).

Snacks are key for kids. Gorp ("good ole raisins and peanuts" or "granola oats raisins and peanuts") makes an energy-packed, quick snack any time of day and is especially tasty if you add M&Ms. Energy/breakfast/granola bars are good. Chocolate bars make for a good quick break. Dried fruit is a nice treat, and it can do double duty as dinner desert if boiled. Powdered drink mixes are another treat. Boil water in your pot for soup packets, ramen, or tea or hot chocolate on cold afternoons or nights. Jiffy Pop is fun over a campstove.

Breakfast can be as involved as you want. I prefer quick meals (cereal with powdered milk, raisins, granola bars), but sometimes pancakes are unbeatable, especially if you've picked fresh blueberries to stir into the mix, and hash browns are awesome in the woods. Some people like instant oatmeal or cream of wheat – I say add lots of brown sugar and raisins.

Lunch can be simple: hard cheeses, crackers or Rye Krisps or pita bread, peanut butter and honey, candy bars, energy bars, nuts, fruit or dried fruit. On cold or wet days, heat up some water for ramen, soup, or tea.

For dinner, pasta (with tomato or cheese sauces or pesto), potatoes, beans (if well soaked), rice, and especially mac and cheese are excellent one pot meals (add lots of fresh or dried veggies and spice well; add canned tuna for protein). Carrots, onions, green pepper, and potatoes travel pretty well at least for a couple days. There are few limits on desserts, so you can have the easy ones like pudding and fruit or more difficult ones like cake, pie, and brownies.

Favorite Trail Meals:

Breakfast
☐ _____
☐ _____
☐ _____

Lunch
☐ _____
☐ _____
☐ _____

Dinner
☐ _____
☐ _____
☐ _____

Most meals can be stored in separately marked ziploc bags. Freeze dried food offers many choices, unlike the old days, but is more expensive than staples like rice and mac and cheese. You really need only one pot (with lid) for cooking.

☐ Spices and oil. Spice Box. Salt and pepper are good, but you can be creative with spices, even with something as simple as mac and cheese. Think about packing cumin, curry, cinnamon, oregano, basil, cayenne pepper, chili powder, garlic powder, dried onion, Bacos, dried milk, bouillon cubes, and your other favorites. Experiment, remembering that most things taste good outdoors, but it is possible to overdo it. Some people caution against using old film containers, but I like them since they are sized just right for spices and can be marked with a piece of masking tape.

☐ Waterproof boots and socks (wool outer socks with synthetic fiber liner socks or special hiking socks that do not need liners). If canoeing, you may want river sandals or old tennis shoes (though the shoes stay wet). The type of boot you get depends on the type of backpacking you'll be doing and loads you'll be carrying. Go to a good outdoor store since the boots are one of the most important pieces of equipment you will have.

☐ Extra pair of dry and comfortable shoes or sandals for around the campsite.

☐ Extra socks. Wool stays warm when wet and wicks moisture away. Some new wool blends are also pretty comfortable; they're not as itchy as the old ragg wool socks. Man-made materials are also pretty good, but cotton is not because it gets soggy and can chafe.

☐ Wool sweater.

☐ Clothing as the weather requires. Layering is best in cool weather. Have clothes that keep you warm when wet (synthetic fibers), and have dry clothes for around the campsite, because you will get wet. The layer closest to your skin should wick away moisture. The middle layers insulate, like synthetic fleece or a wool sweater. The outer layer or shell protects from wind and rain. Remember pants, shorts, underwear, swimsuit, small towel or one of those super-absorbent ones, shirts and T-shirts, warm cap, and extra bandannas. In cold weather, add long underwear (synthetic fibers, not cotton, will keep you warmer), gloves, hats, and appropriate outerwear.

☐ Backpack. Internal vs. external frame. The type of pack you get depends on the hiking you are doing, climate, and trail conditions. If you are loading up for a long summertime hike on marked trails, an external frame pack can hold a ton of gear. Internal frame packs rest right against your back, fitting your movements better, but they may be a bit harder to load. Many people now prefer internal frame packs for shorter trips, and they can be very comfortable.

With any pack, make sure the suspension system works well and comfortably. A padded hip belt is a must, since it will bear most of the load. Look for padded shoulder straps and a mesh back for air circulation.

☐ Sleeping bag in waterproof stuff sack (use a garbage bag inside the stuff sack for insurance). The sleeping bag should be rated for the weather you may encounter.

Summer Clothing List

☐ _____
☐ _____
☐ _____
☐ _____
☐ _____
☐ _____
☐ _____

Fall and Winter Clothing List

☐ _____
☐ _____
☐ _____
☐ _____
☐ _____
☐ _____
☐ _____

☐ Air mattress or foam pad.

☐ Straps to attach gear. How to pack. Pack everything you want to keep dry in garbage bags (one inside the sleeping bag stuff sack, another in the bottom pack compartment for clothes). If you pack like this, and your backpack keeps things relatively dry, you may be able to do without a pack cover.

For river trips, you may want to buy "dry bags" to keep your things dry. Backpacks should be loaded with the heaviest things (extra water, heavy food) close to your back and relatively low in the pack. Sleeping bags go on the bottom, either lashed on or in the lower compartment.

Tents may be lashed to the top, though you may want to pack the heavier parts lower. Mid-weight gear goes more toward the upper and outer areas of the main storage areas. Lightweight stuff on top. Outside pockets are handy for water bottle, maps, raingear, sunscreen, snacks, insect repellent, camera, binoculars, knife, and first aid kit.

☐ Trekking poles. In the old days, people would find a large branch near the trail to use as a walking stick. Nowadays, there are high tech trekking poles. Any walking stick will help you balance on downhills and reduce the strain on your knees.

☐ Stove (that you know works and that you know how to work), fuel canisters or bottles.

☐ Large pot with lid plus smaller pot for dessert or tea, stirring spoon, ladle, and spatula.

☐ Cup and bowl (you don't need plates for most meals anyway so you can just use a sturdy plastic cup or bowl. Insulated cups work well. A canoe paddle can serve as a cutting board in a pinch).

☐ Spoon (you don't need a fork or a knife other than your pocketknife).

☐ Potholder (a bandanna, or pliers on a multipurpose tool).

☐ Biodegradable soap and pot scrubber (Scotchgard, not steel wool, which disintegrates).

☐ Trash bags.

☐ Trowel for digging latrine. If canoeing, you'll also need the "of course" stuff: canoe, paddles (plus spare), life jackets, yoke and pads for portaging, repair kit, waterproof bags for your gear. If fishing, bring your gear. For kayaking, there is specialized gear, like a paddling helmet, paddling jacket, spray skirt, and dry bag for gear. Climbing has a whole different set of equipment. And winter camping requires more of everything.

Trail Games and Activities

Making the outdoors fun for kids means going at their pace and looking at the woods through their eyes – and lots of snacks. Sit next to them. If they are young, draw their attention to the ripples in the creek, the wind in the leaves, the reflection of the sun, and the smell of the pines. Listen to what is around you and to what your children are saying. Here are a few of the countless ways to explore and enjoy the trail:

☐ Sit or stop. With older children, you can have them sit silently, either at a resting place on the trail, at the campsite, or even a little apart from the site. They will be able to focus on hearing the wind, leaves, and animals. The length of silent time depends on your child's age, but a minute per year is a good rough guide.

☐ "Talk about it." Sit in a circle and pass an object around. It can be a rock, stick, piece of moss, feather, sand. Everyone talks about the object for 30 seconds. You can say whatever you want about it. Someone may talk about how it got where it was. Another person might talk about what it is. Someone may talk about what it could be, while another person makes up a story about the object.

☐ Tree ID. Blindfold your child with a bandanna. Lead him to a tree and let him "discover" the tree without looking at it, by smell and feel. Help move his hands over the bark, roots, branches, and leaves. Then, lead him away and take off the blindfold. Let your child see if he can now find "his" tree. Then, you do it. A word about birch trees. Birch trees have beautiful, papery bark. Sometimes you can find pieces of it on the ground. That's fine, and it's fun for kids to play with and peel apart, but never peel birch bark off the birch tree. As we were told at camp, it's like peeling the skin off your arm.

☐ Trail Blazer. Let your child lead down the trail.

☐ Trivia games. This is good for snack breaks. Children can earn dried fruit pieces (we call this "Fruit Bowl") by correctly answering your

Quiet Places

☐ _____

☐ _____

☐ _____

☐ _____

☐ _____

questions (my kids want "Candy Bowl"). Gear questions to your child's age, interests, and what you would like them to remember or learn (sports trivia, history, state capitals, tree identification, math problem, name that tune).

☐ Scavenger Hunt or "Trailseeker." Ask your children to find a twig, pine cone, flat rock, something smooth, something rough, something red, black, white, gray, a feather, something wet, something dry.

☐ Hide and Seek. Like "scavenger hunt," hide and seek is a good choice for younger children around a campsite (with some limits on how far they can go to avoid the game turning into "search and rescue").

☐ Cloud gazing. Stargazing. Bird watching. Drawing and keeping journals. Photo assignment. Cards.

Favorite Trail Games

☐ _____

☐ _____

☐ _____

☐ _____

☐ _____

The Sports *Checklist*

Sports do not build character. They reveal it.

– *Heywood Hale Broun*

People assume dads know all about sports history (like best players by position) and sports how-to (like how to throw a ball).

And it's true that some of my friends can spend hours watching a game, talking about where the pro players went to college, their stats, and what kind of season they're having. While I've learned a lot through ESPN, I don't have that detailed, in-depth, hard-earned knowledge developed through hours of following different sports. Like many parents, weekends are filled with soccer coaching, taking care of things around the house, and running errands, so it's hard to justify (at least to my wife) watching a lot of sports on TV to develop the "expertise" that my friends have. (It's also tough to explain to my wife why flipping channels is actually normal.)

Even so, dads should know some sports history basics to talk about with our children (and friends). The great part about sports history is that almost any position is defensible. No one will laugh if you say the '75 Reds were the best baseball team ever. Even a semi-indefensible position can be okay if it reflects hometown bias (within reason).

On the "how to" side, throwing a ball outside with his son or daughter is a father's privilege and joy. We should go out and teach our children the basics, even if they are not all-star quarterbacks or have no interest in watching the NCAA Final Four. But if they can learn a few skills and sportsmanship with it, well, as Plato, one of ancient Greece's MVPs ("Most Valuable Philosopher"), said, "never discourage anyone who continually makes progress, no matter how slow." And as Mark Twain said, and he could have applied this to your child playing on a local soccer team, "It's not the size of the dog in the fight, it's the size of the fight in the dog."

☑ Signature Sporting Events

☐ **1980** "Miracle on Ice." US Olympic Hockey Team, Lake Placid, New York. The US team was seeded 7th out of 12 teams at Lake Placid. The Soviet team was the best in the world. Somehow, miraculously, the US team defeated the vaunted USSR team, 4-3, in the semifinals. The US went on to beat Finland in the finals for the gold. Those who watched will always remember the excitement and "Do you believe in miracles!"

☐ **1941** Joe DiMaggio's 56 game hitting streak. DiMaggio's hitting streak in the summer of 1941, the same year Ted Williams hit .406, captured an entire nation's imagination.

☐ **1960** Wilma Rudolph's three gold medals at the Rome Olympics (100, 200 meters sprints, 400 meter relay). Rudolph overcame polio and poverty to achieve success.

☐ **2000** Women's World Cup Championship with USA defeating China on penalty kicks.

☐ **2002** Underdog New England Patriots upset St. Louis Rams in Super Bowl XXXVI (why can't they just call it "36"?) with a dramatic 48-yard field goal as time expired. The Patriots declined individual player introductions and ran onto the field as a team. (You could probably name your hometown team's greatest victory here and make a pretty good case for it on this list.)

Most Memorable Games We've Seen

☐ _____

☐ _____

☐ _____

☐ _____

☐ _____

# Baseball

Best Baseball Players Ever

SPORTS NOTE: The home team is listed second in a box score. The home team usually wears white.

Ingrained in our country's culture, baseball takes its place alongside apple pie and Mom. Here is my chart on the best baseball players, by position (relief pitchers not included). I included Negro League players, but blacks being barred from playing in the major leagues for many years prevented us from seeing all the best players on a level playing field. (All stats current as of end of 2011 season.)

▼ First Base – Lou Gehrig (the "Iron Horse")

New York Yankees, 1923-1939.

WHY:

- 3rd all time career slugging percentage (.632, just behind Babe Ruth and Ted Williams).
- 4th all-time career RBI total (1,995).
- Second longest streak of consecutive games played (2,130), after Cal Ripken.
- Gehrig had a .340 career batting average (13th), 493 homers (26th), and was a two-time MVP.

BUT YOU CAN'T ARGUE WITH: There is no debate about Gehrig being the best first baseman and one of the best players of all time. But, if you need a few others to argue about for backups:

Jimmie Foxx, most of career with Philadelphia Athletics/Boston Red Sox 1925–42, 1944–1945, three-time MVP, two Triple Crowns, 5th in slugging percentage (.609), 7th in RBIs (1,922), and 17th in homers (534).

Hank Greenberg, Detroit Tigers 1930, 1933-1941, 1945-1947 (Pirates 1947), two-time MVP, 7th in slugging percentage (.605), and 125+ RBIs six times. Greenberg's playing career was shortened by his military service.

Walter "Buck" Leonard, Brooklyn Royal Giants 1933, Homestead Grays 1934-1950. With Grays, won nine pennants in a row and was one of Negro League all-time home run leaders.

▼ Second Base – Joe Morgan

1963-1984, with heyday of career with Cincinnati Reds ('72-'79).

WHY:
- Five Gold Gloves.
- Two MVPs.
- Stole 40+ bases nine straight seasons.
- 268 home runs.
- Morgan was a key member of those championship Reds teams in the 1970s.

BUT YOU CAN'T ARGUE WITH: Many consider the best second baseman to be **Nap Lajoie,** Philadelphia and Cleveland 1902-1916. Lajoie by reputation is always ranked as one of the best defensive second basemen ever, with a good bat (.338 avg., 16th all time, and 3,242 hits, 12th all time).

Our Favorite Players

1B	_____
2B	_____
SS	_____
3B	_____
LF	_____
CF	_____
RF	_____
C	_____
RHP	_____
LHP	_____
Bench	_____
Bench	_____
Bench	_____

Jackie Robinson, Brooklyn Dodgers 1947–1956, is remembered for breaking the color barrier in major league baseball, but he was also a great player, earning Rookie of the Year honors, an MVP award, batting title, and three fielding titles.

Two-time MVP and two-time triple crown, **Rogers Hornsby,** St. Louis 1915–1937, whose .358 career average is second to Cobb and whose .577 slugging percentage is 11th alltime.

◆ Third Base – Mike Schmidt

Philadelphia Phillies, 1972–1989.

WHY:
- Three-time MVP.
- 15th all-time in home runs (548).
- 10 Gold Gloves.
- Schmidt set the standard for third basemen offensively and defensively.

BUT YOU CAN'T ARGUE WITH: **Brooks Robinson,** Baltimore Orioles 1955–1977, known as one of the best defensive third basemen ever (16 Gold Gloves).

◆ Shortstop – Honus Wagner

Louisville Colonels/Pittsburgh Pirates, 1897–1917.

WHY:
- Eight NL batting titles and .327 average.

- 21st all-time in RBIs (1,732).
- 7th all-time in hits (3,415).
- 722 stolen bases (9th all-time), while, according to baseball records, getting caught only 15 times.
- Wagner was reputed to be an excellent fielder and is considered one of the all-time greats.

BUT YOU CAN'T ARGUE WITH: **Cal Ripken**, Baltimore Orioles 1981–2001. Ripken played a record 2,632 straight games (1982-98), won two MVPs, and was a 19 time All Star.

A great defensive shortstop known as the "Wizard of Oz," **Ozzie Smith**, St. Louis Cardinals (early in career with Padres), 1978–1996, won 13 Gold Gloves.

▼ Left Field – Ted Williams (the "Splendid Splinter")

Boston Red Sox, 1939-1942, 1946-1960 (missing five seasons for his military service in WWII and Korea), the best hitter in baseball.

WHY:
- Hit .406 in 1941, the last .400 hitter in Major League Baseball (but Buck Leonard hit .410 in 1947 for the Homestead Grays).
- First all-time in on base percentage (.482).
- Second all-time to Ruth in slugging percentage (.634).
- 5th in career average (.344).
- 21 home runs (18th).
- 4th in walks (2,019).
- 14th in RBIs (1,839).
- Two Triple Crowns.
- Two-time MVP.

BUT YOU CAN'T ARGUE WITH: Stan "The Man" Musial, St. Louis Cardinals 1941–1963, three time MVP, 4th in hits (3,630); 5th in RBIs (1,951); 21st in batting average (.331) and 17th in slugging (.559). Musial was a 24 time All Star, seven time NL batting champion, hit over .300 17 times, and hit 475 home runs in his career.

▼ Center Field – Willie Mays

New York, then San Francisco Giants, 1951–1952, 1954–1973
(with a stint in the Army 1952–1953 and NY Mets 1972–1973).

WHY:
- 12 Gold Gloves.
- 20 time All Star.
- Two-time MVP.
- 1st in outfield putouts.
- 4th in home runs (660).
- 9th in RBIs (1,903).
- 10th in hits (3,283).
- 18th in slugging percentage (.557), with .302 batting average.
- Mays stands out here, among some worthy competition. He is immortalized in the 1954 World Series photo of his over the head catch of Vic Wertz's drive to deep center.

BUT YOU CAN'T ARGUE WITH: Picking a starting center fielder may be the toughest call of all positions. Look at the competition:

James "Cool Papa" Bell, St. Louis Stars, Kansas City Monarchs, Chicago American Giants, Pittsburgh Crawfords, Homestead Grays, 1922–1950. Bell was among the best Negro League players ever, reputed to be one of the fastest ever to play the game, hit over .300 regularly and over .400 a few times.

Joe DiMaggio, New York Yankees 1936–1942, 1946–1951, whose record 56 game hitting streak held the country spellbound in 1941, was a member of nine World Series champion teams. The "Yankee Clipper" ranks 10th on the all time list for slugging percentage with .579 (.325 career batting average).

Mickey Mantle, New York Yankees 1951–1968, arguably better than DiMaggio, was a three time MVP who hit 536 career home runs (16th) and ranks 19th on the career slugging percentage list with .557.

Ty Cobb, Detroit Tigers 1905–1926, Philadelphia Athletics 1927–1928, a record-setting .367 lifetime batting average, with 12 batting titles and eight slugging titles, and 2nd in runs with 2,245. Though nasty personally, "The Georgia Peach" hit .420 in 1911, was 6th in RBIs with 1,938, 2nd in hits to Pete Rose (4,256) with 4,191, and stole 892 bases (4th).

⬥ Right Field – Babe Ruth

Boston Red Sox, 1914–1919, New York Yankees, 1920–1934,
Boston Braves, 1935

WHY:
- 3rd in home runs (714) to Aaron and Bonds.
- 1st in slugging percentage (.690).
- 8th in batting average (.342).
- 2nd in RBIs (2,213).
- 3rd in walks (2,062).
- "The Sultan of Swat" energized the game and made it
  massively popular.

BUT YOU CAN'T ARGUE WITH: **Hank Aaron,** Milwaukee/Atlanta Braves 1954–1974, Milwaukee Brewers 1975–1976. Three-time Gold Glover, "Hammerin" Hank Aaron hit the most home runs ever— 755 until Barry Bonds surpassed him with 762. He was named to 24 All-Star teams, and ranks 4th in career runs (2,174, tied with Ruth). 1st in RBIs (2,297), and 3rd in hits (3,771). For a time I debated starting Aaron as my right fielder, but the overwhelming consensus among baseball experts is that Ruth was one of the best players of all time, if not the best, not just one of the best right fielders.

Catcher – Yogi Berra

New York Yankees, 1946–1963, Mets 1965.

WHY:
- Three-time MVP.
- 15 time All Star.
- 358 home runs with .285 average.
- 10 championship teams.
- Known for his "Yogiisms" like "It ain't over til it's over," "It's déjà vu all over again," and "You can observe a lot by watching," Berra was one of the all-time greats.

BUT YOU CAN'T ARGUE WITH: **Johnny Bench,** Cincinnati Reds, 1967–1983, was a two-time MVP, 14 time All Star, and earned 10 Gold Gloves. For me, it was a tough call between Berra and Bench. I'd rank them 1 and 1A.

Josh Gibson, Homestead Grays, Pittsburgh Crawfords 1930–1946, was considered the greatest slugger in the Negro Leagues with at least 800

HRs and four batting championships and a reported 75 HRs in one season.

Roy Campanella, Brooklyn Dodgers 1948–1957, three-time MVP helped his team win five pennants and a world championship.

▼ Right-Handed Pitcher – Walter Johnson ("Big Train")

Washington Senators, 1907–1927.

WHY:
- 1st in shutouts (110).
- 2nd in wins (417) to Cy Young.
- 3rd in complete games (531) (and 4th in losses with 279).
- 9th in strikeouts (3,508).
- 7th in ERA (2.17).
- Three pitching Triple Crowns.
- Won 20 or more games 12 times.

BUT YOU CAN'T ARGUE WITH: Satchel Paige, Cleveland Indians 1948–1949, St. Louis Browns 1951–1953, Kansas City Athletics 1965, actually started his career in MLB at age 42 after a stellar career in the Negro Leagues (1926–1947) with the Kansas City Monarchs, among other teams, where he won 124 games and was, by reputation, a superb pitcher and one of the hardest throwers in Negro League history.

Christy Mathewson, New York Giants 1900–1916, had a 373-188 record; 2.13 ERA (6th), 2,502 strikeouts, and two Triple Crowns. His wins place him 3rd all time. He won 20 or more games 13 times, 30 or more four times; and threw 79 shutouts (3rd behind Johnson and Alexander).

Cy Young, Cleveland Spiders 1890–1898, St. Louis 1899–1900, Boston Red Sox 1901-1908, Cleveland Indians 1909-1911, Boston Braves 1911, pitched a record 7,356 innings with a 511-316 won-loss record and 2.63 career earned run average. His 511 wins, 749 complete games, and 316 losses are all first in their categories. Young's 76 shutouts rank fourth all time. The annual award for best pitcher in each league is named after him.

Grover Cleveland Alexander, Philadelphia/Chicago 1911–1930, had 2,198 strikeouts, a 373-208 won-loss record (3rd all-time in wins), and a 2.56 ERA. Two Triple Crowns. He had an NL record 90 shutouts (2nd) and 437 complete games.

Other Notables include:

Bob Gibson, St. Louis, 1959–1975, had 3,117 strikeouts (14th), a 2.91 ERA, and a 251-174 record.

Tom Seaver, New York Mets/Cincinnati Reds, 1967–1986, had 3,640 strikeouts (6th), a 2.86 ERA, and a 311-205 record.

Nolan Ryan, Mets 1966-1971, Angels 1972–1979, Astros 1980–1988, Rangers 1989–1993, with a record seven no-hitters and a record 5,714 strikeouts.

◆ Left-Handed Pitcher – Sandy Koufax

Los Angeles Dodgers, 1955–1966.

WHY:
- Three-time Cy Young winner.
- Three Triple Crowns.
- MVP and two time World Series MVP.
- 2nd in opponents' batting average against (.205).

Although his career was short, Koufax' numbers are impressive. A 165-87 record, matched with 2,396 strikeouts and a 2.76 ERA evidenced his dominance. From 1961–1966, he was 129-47 (2.19 ERA) with three no-hitters, a perfect game, an 0.95 ERA in four World Series, and three Cy Young Awards.

BUT YOU CAN'T ARGUE WITH: There is really no debate about Koufax, but another great lefty was **Lefty Grove,** Philadelphia/Boston 1925–1941, who went 300-141, with a 3.06 ERA, with a 31-4 season in 1931.

☑ The Three Best Major League Baseball Teams Ever

☐ **1. 1927 New York Yankees,** with Ruth and Gehrig. The team was called "Murderer's Row" for their outstanding hitting, had an amazing regular season record of 110-44 (in the older days, the season was 154 games, not 162), and swept a good Pittsburgh team in the World Series.

☐ **2. 1939 Yankees** led the league in hitting and pitching, went 106-45, and swept Cincinnati in the World Series.

☐ **3. 1975 Cincinnati Reds'** championship team included Joe Morgan, Johnny Bench, Pete Rose, and Ken Griffey, defeating the Boston Red Sox in seven games (and won again in 1976).

ALSO GREAT: 1935 Pittsburgh Crawfords, known as the best Negro League team of all time, included CF Cool Papa Bell, C Josh Gibson, P Satchel Paige, and 1B Oscar Charleston; 1998 New York Yankees (114 regular season wins); 1970 Baltimore Orioles; 1961 New York Yankees.

☑ Most Dominant Baseball Team Historically

Over time, the New York Yankees have dominated major league baseball. With 40 pennants and 27 World Series championships, the Yankees may be the best sports franchise ever. The 1947–1962 teams won 10 World Series over 16 seasons (losing game sevens in three of those years) and had DiMaggio, Mantle, and Berra. The 1936–43 teams with DiMaggio won six World Series.

SPORTS NOTE: The "triple crown" in baseball is the league leader in batting average, home runs, and runs batted in. There have been nine triple crowns in the American League (Ted Williams won twice), and five triple crowns in the National League (Rogers Hornsby won twice). If someone refers to the "pitching" triple crown in baseball, it means wins, strikeouts, and earned run average. Most of the time "triple crown" in baseball refers to batting. The "triple crown" in horse racing is the winner of three races: Belmont Stakes, Preakness Stakes, and the Kentucky Derby. Eleven horses have won the triple crown, including *War Admiral* (1937), *Whirlaway* (1941), *Secretariat* (1973), and, most recently, *Affirmed* (1978).

✓ Three Baseball Rules

If you know these rules, you will look like you understand baseball.

⬛ **Ground Rule Double.** A ground rule double is called when a fair ball bounces over the outfield fence out of play or is touched by a fan. The batter and any base runners advance two bases.

⬛ **Balk.** When a pitcher stops his motion toward home and instead throws to a base, it is a "balk" and all runners advance a base. An umpire will also call a balk when the pitcher does not come to a stop at the set position or pauses in his delivery to the plate or a whole bunch of other reasons if the moves tend to trick a baserunner.

⬛ **Infield Fly Rule.** The infield fly rule comes into play when a fly ball is hit to the infield with runners on 1st and 2nd base or 1st, 2nd, and 3rd, with fewer than two outs. (Remember "1-2-1-2-3, not 2" for the runners on 1st and 2nd or 1st, 2nd, and 3rd with fewer than two outs.) The umpire calls "infield fly". The batter will be out, whether or not the ball is caught, and base runners are not required to run to the next base, though they may advance at their own risk.

☑ Three Useful Baseball Terms

⬤ **Infield In.** If there is a runner in scoring position and the score is close, the infielders may move closer to home plate so that they have a better chance to get an out on the runner trying to go home. The risk of having the "infield in" is that the batter may loft a ball between the outfielders and the infielders who are "playing in."

⬤ **Pitchout.** If the fielding team thinks a runner may steal, the manager may signal to his catcher to call for a pitchout, a pitch away from the batter. The batter cannot hit the ball, and the catcher is in a better position to throw out a runner trying to steal.

⬤ **Squeeze Play.** The batter bunts the ball while the runner on third base attempts to score. If the runner begins running to home plate before the batter makes contact with the ball, it is called a suicide squeeze. If the runner waits for the ball to be bunted before running, it is called a safety squeeze.

SPORTS NOTE: In baseball, a runner "in scoring position" means a runner on second or third base.

✔ Baseball Statistics and Keeping Score

☐ Batting Statistics

	Batting Average (Avg.)	Runs Batted In (RBI)	On Base Percentage (OBP)	Slugging Percentage (SLG)
What it is	Traditional measure of hitting.	Measures how effectively a batter scores runs.	Percentage of time player reaches base.	Measure of total bases.
How to calculate	Number of hits divided by number of at bats.	RBI credited when a runner scores due to batter's hit, walk, sacrifice bunt or sacrifice fly, or reaching base on a fielder's choice.	Add hits, walks, hit by pitch. Divide result by the sum of at bats, walks, hit by pitch, and sacrifice flies.	Total number of all bases divided by at bats.
Finer points	Does not account for walks or extra base hits. .300 is the standard in the major leagues for a respectable hitter.	Can be credited with RBI on error if would have scored anyway. Depends a lot on where batter hits in the lineup.	Gives a better picture of how often a hitter reaches base.	Adding OBP and SLG gives you OPS or on-base plus slugging, which tells you how often the batter reaches and how effective he is.

☐ Pitching Statistics

	Earned Run Average (ERA)	Saves
What it is	Traditional way to measure a pitcher's effectiveness.	Relief pitching statistic for holding a lead.
How to calculate and finer points	Multiply total number of earned runs by nine. Divide result by total innings pitched. Earned runs are runs charged against the pitcher such as for hits, walks, stolen bases, and hit batters but do not include runners that reach base on errors or who would not have scored but for the error. For pitchers, strikeouts per nine innings is another useful statistic.	To earn a save, relief pitcher must be the last pitcher for the winning team and must have (1) entered the game with a lead of no more than three runs, and pitched at least one inning, or (2) entered the game with the tying run on base, at bat, or on deck, or (3) pitched effectively for three innings. The third qualification is at the discretion of the official scorer.

☑ Keeping Score in Baseball

Baseball positions are also designated by number, which comes into play if you are keeping score (that is, tracking the game out by out on a scorecard):

1 = pitcher or P
2 = catcher or C
3 = 1st base or 1B
4 = 2nd base or 2B
5 = 3rd base or 3B
6 = shortstop or SS (this is the confusing one because the shortstop plays between #4 and #5)
7 = left field or LF

8 = center field of CF

9 = right field or RF

DH = designated hitter or DH (American League only)

For example, if the batter hits a ground ball to the shortstop, who throws to first and gets the runner out, the play is marked down on the scorecard as 6-3. If there were a runner on first, and the ball was hit to the shortstop (6), the shortstop throws to the second baseman (4), the second baseman throws to the first baseman (3), and the runner and batter are thrown out, then it is a classic 6-4-3 double play.

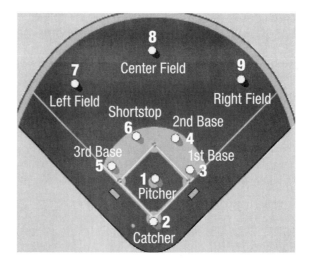

REALITY CHECK: Using a scorecard is easier than it looks. Print out some blanks with instructions from the internet and follow the game. As long as you can tell what your notations mean, you're keeping score. This is fun for kids.

✔ How to Throw a Baseball

☐ **Grip the ball** with the middle and index fingers across or along the seams on the top and the thumb under the ball. (Younger children may not be able to grip this way yet.)

☐ **Find the target.** Look right at where you want the ball to go, cock the arm back, with the elbow bent, and twist a little bit back with weight on back leg.

☐ **Pivot, pushing off** The rear foot, and step forward while throwing the ball overhand or three quarters overhand. Keep eyes on target. Think about throwing "through" the target.

☐ **Follow through** (continue with the motion). Sometimes players, shortstops especially, will make a sidearm throw to another fielder covering a base. This is for quick tosses and (usually) short distances. Most players, though, should concentrate on the three quarters overhand throw to get the most power and to minimize wear and tear on the arm. Young pitchers should be working on "fastballs" (location, location, location) and then changeups. Curves and sliders can wait until they are older and have a good pitching coach.

> **REALITY CHECK:** Even with fastballs, the key for younger players is getting the pitch in the strike zone and not worrying about trying to overpower the hitters. It is also important to limit their pitch count if they pitch in a league so as not to stress their arms at a young age. If your child is serious about pitching, a few lessons from a qualified pitching coach will help make sure that they learn the mechanics correctly from the get go, before they start getting bad habits.

☑ Some Pitches and What They Do

Four Seam Fastball	The index and middle fingers cross the seams. This is the classic fastball, with a four seam rotation, where the pitcher throws it as hard as he can.	
Two Seam Fastball	The index and middle fingers grip along the seams. The pitcher throws it hard and fast, and the ball will have some "movement" on it.	
Split Fingered Fastball	Thrown with fingers "split" wider and results in ball dropping more than a straight fastball.	
Cut Fastball	The pitcher puts more pressure on his middle finger when throwing, "cutting" it through the ball, and the ball "cuts" or veers away at the end.	

Sinker	A fastball that "sinks" or "tails" off. Results in a lot of grounders because batters tend to hit the top of the ball.
Slider	Like a curveball, a slider "breaks," but it is faster than a curveball.
Curve	The classic "breaking ball," the curve drops down over the plate in a "12 to 6" motion for a good curveball. Slower than a fastball, the curve is an off-speed pitch.
Change Up	An off-speed pitch, the changeup is thrown with the same arm motion as a fastball to fool the batter. Because of the way the pitcher holds the ball, deeper in the hand or with more fingers on it, or by circling the thumb and index finger, the ball comes out more slowly (by a few miles per hour) and upsets the batter's timing.
Knuckleball	There are few knuckleball pitchers. They grip the ball with pressure on their fingertips, and the ball "dances."

✔ How to Hit a Baseball

Hitting a baseball is not easy. Patience and practice are key when teaching your children. Use a T-ball tee or soft toss underhand with a tennis ball for a while when your children are first learning. After a while – and it can be a couple seasons – they'll be able to hit overhand pitching.

☐ **Rule number one:** Keep your eye on the ball. This means watch the ball, but as hitters move up through different leagues, they find that you really cannot "see" the ball every second until it hits the bat. The key - follow the ball with your eyes.

☐ **Get set.** Grip the bat hands together (one on top of the other) near the bottom knob but not all the way at the bottom. Younger children should "choke up" on the bat – leave some space at the bottom, maybe an inch or two above the knob. Choking up gives more control. (Bottom hand is the arm closer to pitcher - sometimes you see young children reverse their hands.)

☐ **Stand at the plate.** Be able to touch the outside corner of the plate with the bat, feet shoulder-width apart, toes of both feet pointing at the plate. If you draw a line across the front of the toes, they would point straight out to the pitcher – that's for a neutral stance. If the foot closer to the pitcher is further away from the plate, the stance is "open."

Life grants nothing to us mortals without hard work.
– Horace

SPORTS NOTE: A "checked swing" is when a batter holds up his swing – that is, the bat does not go past the front edge of home plate.

☐ **Hold the bat up** with hands chest level (some hitters hold the hands higher, shoulder level). The bat should be at no more than a 45 degree angle to the ground and should be pulled back in the direction of the back shoulder. Weight should be slightly on the back leg.

☐ **When you see the pitch** and are ready to swing, rock weight from back leg to front, bring the hands forward, pivot the back foot toward the pitcher (toes pointing to pitcher) while twisting shoulders and hips into the pitch, swinging the bat through the ball and extending the arms. (The strike zone is from the knees to between the belt and shoulders, that is, about midchest.)

☐ **Follow through with the bat.** Drop, don't sling, the bat and run to first.

☐ **Remember that even the best** major league hitters hit safely about three times out of ten (but they're facing major league pitching).

REALITY CHECK: When we first began learning baseball, my children hit a rubber ball off a tee, and, like many children, sometimes hit the tee and not the ball. Then they played for hours in the backyard with each other and practiced fielding, throwing, and hitting many afternoons with my wife at the elementary school ballfield. They progressed to underhand soft toss then to overhand slow pitches. They've both been playing Little League. And, on vacation after a day at the beach and before we would go to Cape Cod League baseball games in the evenings, we would go to a local batting cage for fun. They started off five years ago [that was back in 2003] hitting in the wiffle ball cage with oversize bats. About four years ago, they went in the 35 mph Little League cage, hit well, and after persuading me moved up to the 55 mph Babe Ruth League cage where they were able to hit pretty consistently. From trying to hit off a tee to hitting 55 mph pitches a couple years later seemed like pretty fair progress.

☑ How to Catch a Baseball

☐ **Rule number one:** Keep your eye on the ball.

☐ **Be ready for a ball** hit to you. Think about where you will throw it before the play begins. Being mentally prepared on the play is key. But be sure to focus on catching the ball first.

☐ **Get set.** Feet shoulder width apart, arms loose. For a ground ball, keep knees bent, get to the ball, face the ball head on, keep glove down and open, foot on glove side should be slightly forward. For a fly ball, run to where you think it is going while watching it. Call for the ball ("Mine!") if you are in the best position to make the play. Get ready to catch it.

☐ **For a ground ball,** move into position, keeping the glove (and your tailgate) down, watch the ball into the glove. Use both hands – the throwing hand should help trap the ball in the glove. For a fly ball, glove should be in the air, open to the ball. Watch the ball into the glove, and use the throwing hand to help trap the ball in the glove.

☐ **Look where you are going** to throw it and step into the throw.

REALITY CHECK: If you've been to Little League games, you've seen it - the ball going under the player's glove. My children have spent a lot of practice time making sure to keep the glove down.

☑ Coaching Tips for Coaches and Parents for Any Sport

▶ **Breathe and relax** (you and your child).

▶ **The goal is to have fun,** especially for younger children (these are games), and to learn sportsmanship, skills, and teamwork.

▶ **It's a lot more fun** when you're winning, and the key to winning is simple in concept but difficult in commitment: practice. Practicing on all facets of the game builds skill, situational awareness, and confidence. Have your child visualize hitting the ball, making the basket, kicking the goal (visualizing helps in any sport).

▶ **Praise good effort.** Applaud good plays on both teams.

▶ **Think about whether you need** to make corrections during a game (unless they're for safety) – after a certain age players usually know what they did and are trying to think about a lot of things already. It's hard to focus on the game when people are yelling lots of instructions from the sidelines. When talking to the players, from time to time, get eye level to eye level when instructing.

▶ **Never yell** at the ref or the coach. Never use the word "loser."

▶ **After a game,** ask your child if she had fun.

☑ Football – The Three Best Football Teams Ever

Leaders aren't born. They are made. And they are made just like anything else – through hard work.

– Vince Lombardi

SPORTS NOTE: High school football is played Friday night, college Saturday, and pro Sunday, with one NFL game on Monday night.

☐ **1. 1972 Miami Dolphins.** The only undefeated NFL team (final season record 17-0, including Super Bowl VII win). The Dolphins led the league in scoring (27.5 points per game) and scoring defense (12.2 points per game). The team included stars Bob Griese, Larry Csonka, Jim Kiick, and Mercury Morris under coach Don Shula. Naysayers say the Dolphins had an easy schedule. I say 17 wins in the NFL is 17 wins in the NFL, no matter who you are playing. By the way, the Dolphins won the Super Bowl again the following year.

☐ **2. 1985 Chicago Bears,** 15-1 regular season, defeated New England Patriots 46-10 in the Super Bowl.

☐ **3. 1978 Pittsburgh Steelers,** with Terry Bradshaw, Franco Harris, Lynn Swann, and John Stallworth defeated Dallas 35-31 in the Super Bowl. From 1974 to 1979, the Steelers won four Super Bowls in six seasons. Other good to great football teams include Vince Lombardi's 1967 Green Bay Packers, Joe Montana-Jerry Rice's 1989 San Francisco 49ers, 1990s Dallas Cowboys, and early 2000s New England Patriots.

✔ The All-Time Best Football Players

I'm not an expert, but here are some all-time football greats, pretty much by consensus.

☐ Offense

Position	Player	Second Team
Quarterback	**Joe Montana,** San Francisco 49ers, 1979–92, Kansas City Chiefs, 1993–94. Quarterbacking the 49ers to four Super Bowl wins, eight time All-Pro Montana is the only four time Super Bowl MVP, throwing 122 times with no interceptions in those four games."Joe Cool" simply won games.	**Johnny Unitas,** Baltimore Colts, 1956–72, San Diego Chargers, 1973. **Otto Graham,** Cleveland Browns, 1946–55. **John Elway,** Denver Broncos, 1983-98. **Dan Marino,** Miami Dolphins, 1983-99. **Terry Bradshaw,** Pittsburgh Steelers, 1970–83. **Tom Brady** (New England Patriots, 2000–present) and **Peyton Manning** (Indianapolis Colts, 1998-2011) will join this elite group.
Running Back	**Jim Brown,** Cleveland Browns, 1957–65. Considered one of the best, if not the best, all time. Eight time NFL rushing leader, Nine time Pro Bowler, Brown had 58 100-yard games and an NFL record 5.2 yards per carry.	**Barry Sanders,** Detroit Lions, 1989-98. **Bronko Nagurski,** Chicago Bears, 1930–37, 1943.

SPORTS NOTE ON TEAMWORK:

"The secret is to work less as individuals and more as a team. As a coach, I play not my eleven best but my best eleven."
—Knute Rockne

"There's no 'I' in 'Team'."
—Coaches everywhere

SPORTS NOTE ON FOOTBALL AND LIFE:

"It's not whether you get knocked down. It's whether you get up."
– Vince Lombardi

☐ **Offense** (continued)

Position	Player	Second Team
Running Back	**Walter Payton,** Chicago Bears, 1975–87. Payton gained an NFL record 16,726 yards rushing.	**Gale Sayers,** Chicago Bears, 1965–71. **Eric Dickerson,** Los Angeles Rams, 1983–87, Indianapolis Colts, 1987–91, Los Angeles Raiders, 1992, Atlanta Falcons, 1993.
Wide Receiver	**Jerry Rice,** San Francisco 49ers, 1985–2000, Oakland Raiders, 2001–2004, Seattle Seahawks, 2004.	**Lance Alworth,** San Diego Chargers, 1962–70, Dallas Cowboys, 1971–72.
Wide Receiver	**Don Hutson,** Green Bay Packers, 1935–45.	**Raymond Berry,** Baltimore Colts, 1955–67.
Tight End	**John Mackey,** Baltimore Colts, 1963–71, San Diego Chargers, 1972.	**Kellen Winslow,** San Diego Chargers, 1979–87.
Tackle	**Anthony Munoz,** Cincinnati Bengals, 1980–92.	**Art Shell,** Oakland-Los Angeles Raiders, 1968–82.
Tackle	**Forrest Gregg,** Green Bay Packers, 1956, 1958–70, Dallas Cowboys, 1971.	**Roosevelt Brown,** New York Giants, 1953–65.
Guard	**John Hannah,** New England Patriots, 1973–85.	**Gene Upshaw,** Oakland Raiders, 1967–81.
Guard	**Jim Parker,** Baltimore Colts, 1957–67.	**Larry Little,** San Diego Chargers, 1967–68, Miami Dolphins, 1969–80.
Center	**Mike Webster,** Pittsburgh Steelers, 1974–88, Kansas City Chiefs, 1989–90.	**Jim Otto,** Oakland Raiders, 1960–74.

Our Favorite Players

QB _____

RB _____

RB _____

WR _____

WR _____

TE _____

LT _____

RT _____

LG _____

RG _____

C _____

☐ Defense

Position	Player	Second Team
Defensive Tackle	**Joe Greene,** Pittsburgh Steelers, 1969–81.	**Alan Page,** Minnesota Vikings, 1967–78, Chicago Bears, 1978–81. Buck Buchanan, Kansas City Chiefs, 1963-75.
Defensive Tackle	**Bob Lilly,** Dallas Cowboys, 1961–74.	**Merlin Olsen,** Los Angeles Rams, 1962–76.
Defensive End	**Deacon Jones,** Los Angeles Rams, 1961–71, San Diego Chargers, 1972–73, Washington Redskins, 1974.	**Bruce Smith,** Buffalo Bills, 1985–1999, Washington Redskins, 2000–2003.
Defensive End	**Gino Marchetti,** Dallas Texans, 1952, Baltimore Colts, 1953–64, 1966.	**Reggie White,** Philadelphia Eagles, 1985–92, Green Bay Packers, 1993–98, Carolina Panthers, 2000.
Linebacker	**Dick Butkus,** Chicago Bears, 1965–73.	**Jack Lambert,** Pittsburgh Steelers, 1974–84. **Willie Lanier,** Kansas City Chiefs, 1967–77.
Linebacker	**Lawrence Taylor,** New York Giants, 1981–93.	**Chuck Bednarik,** Philadelphia Eagles, 1949–62.
Linebacker	**Ray Nitschke,** Green Bay Packers, 1958–72.	**Jack Ham,** Pittsburgh Steelers, 1971–82. **Mike Singletary,** Chicago Bears, 1981–92.
Comeback	**Dick "Night Train" Lane,** Los Angeles Rams, 1952–53, Chicago Cardinals, 1954–59, Detroit Lions, 1960–65.	**Herb Adderley,** Green Bay Packers, 1961–69, Dallas Cowboys, 1970–72.

Our Favorite Players

DT _____

DT _____

DE _____

DE _____

OLB _____

MLB _____

OLB _____

CB _____

CB _____

S _____

S _____

Position	Player	Second Team
Comeback	**Mel Blount,** Pittsburgh Steelers, 1970-83.	**Deion Sanders,** Atlanta Falcons, 1989–93, San Francisco 49ers, 1994, Dallas Cowboys, 1995–99, Washington Redskins, 2000, Baltimore Ravens, 2004–05.
Safety	**Ronnie Lott,** San Francisco 49ers, 1981–90, Los Angeles Raiders, 1991–92, New York Jets, 1993-94.	**Rod Woodson,** Pittsburgh Steelers, 1987–96, San Francisco 49ers, 1997, Baltimore Ravens 1998–2001.
Safety	**Larry Wilson,** St. Louis Cardinals, 1960–72	**Emlen Tunnell,** New York Giants, 1948–58, Green Bay Packers, 1959–61.

☑ Interesting to Know – NFL Jersey Numbers

- Quarterbacks, Kickers: 1–19
- Running Backs, Defensive Backs: 20–49
- Centers, Linebackers, Cornerbacks: 50–59
- Defensive Linemen, Interior Offensive Linemen: 60–79
- Wide Receivers, Tight Ends: 80–89
- Defensive Linemen, Linebackers: 90–99

✓ Basketball – The Three Best Basketball Teams Ever

☐ **1. Boston Celtics,** 1957–1969, winners of 11 championships in 13 years, led by Bill Russell.

☐ **2. Chicago Bulls,** 1991–1998, winners of six championships, led by Michael Jordan. The 1996 Bulls' record of 72 wins and 10 losses is the all-time best NBA won-loss record.

☐ **3. Los Angeles Lakers,** 1972. This championship team was 69-13 in the regular season. (The 2001 Lakers were also a dominant team and deserve at least honorable mention.)

What you are as a person is far more important than what you are as a basketball player.

– John Wooden

✓ Greatest Basketball Players

My college roommate/basketball fan supreme Joe says there can be no disputing this, and having learned the hard way never to bet against Joe in sports I am going to have to defer to his expertise on this one:

☐ **Five-time MVP Chicago Bulls** (1984–93, 1995–98, Washington Wizards 2001–03) guard Michael Jordan, who won six championships and is the all-time leader in average points per game (30.1), 2nd in steals, 4th in points, and 5th in free throws made.

☐ **Five-time MVP Boston Celtics** (1956–69) center Bill Russell, who led his team to 11 championships.

☑ Basketball Positions

Our Favorite Players

G _____

G _____

F _____

F _____

C _____

☐ **1. Point Guard.** Quarterbacks the team, brings the ball up the floor, passes off to open teammates.

☐ **2. Shooting Guard.** Ballhandling skills with ability to take shots from anywhere on the court.

☐ **3. Small Forward.** Not really small, but sometimes smaller than the power forward. Also must be able to shoot from anywhere on the court.

☐ **4. Power Forward.** Plays closer to the basket than small forward and goes for rebounds.

☐ **5. Center.** Tallest player on the team. Responsible mostly for rebounding.

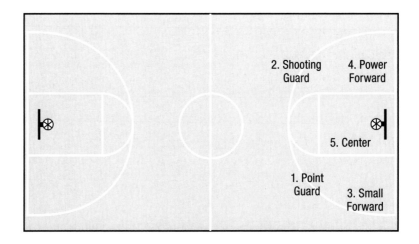

☑ Tabletop Games

☐ Paper Football

Just like you used to play in fourth grade:

☐ Fold a regular sheet of paper in half, lengthwise.
☐ Fold it in half again, lengthwise, so that you have a long, thin piece.
☐ Next, take one of the top corners and fold it down on a diagonal.
☐ Repeat all the way down.
☐ When you get near the bottom, tear off any excess length so that you have about a ¼ inch sticking out. Tuck that into the fold of the paper.

Ready for kickoff!

How to Play: You play on a tabletop, like a school desk. To score a touchdown (and move the ball), lay it flat on the desk. Flick with your index finger. Cross the edge of the desk without falling off for a TD! If it falls off an edge, your opponent gets the ball. If there is doubt about whether the ball crossed the goal line, you take a straight edge or your hand along the edge (without leaning on it) and if it hits the ball, that's a touchdown. If not, your opponent goes.

To kick a field goal, place the ball on a long edge point, either flat side or pointed side facing you, with index finger holding the top of the ball. Flick the ball with your index finger through goalposts to score. For goalposts, your opponent rests his fists on the table, points index fingers in, so that they just touch, and raises thumbs.

☐ Coin Hockey

Take three pennies. Line them up at the edge of a desk or table. Advance the pennies by sliding the center one with your index finger on top, flicking it, and letting it go. Each shot must go between the other two pennies. The other person forms a goal with his index finger and pinky hooked over the edge of the desk.

NOTE ON SPORTSMANSHIP:

"Ability without honor has no value."

– Emerson (after Cicero)

Sportsmanship Tips
- Be humble in victory, gracious in defeat.
- When you score, don't gloat. Act like you've done it before.
- Respect your opponent, your teammates, your coaches, and yourself.

✔ Best College Team Nicknames

☐ Three Best College Team Nicknames

- Delta State University Statesmen, aka Fighting Okra (Cleveland, MS)
- University of Akron Zips (Akron, OH)
- University of Hawaii Rainbow Warriors (Honolulu, HI)

☐ Also Pretty Good College Team Nicknames:

- Bennett College Belles (Greensboro, NC)
- Bluefield State College Big Blues (Bluefield, WV)
- California Maritime Academy Keelhaulers (Vallejo, CA)
- Coastal Carolina University Chanticleers (Conway, SC)
- Connecticut College Camels (New London, CT)
- Furman Paladins (Greenville, SC)
- Kent State University Golden Flashes (Kent, OH)
- Manhattan College Jaspers (Riverdale, NY)
- San Diego State Aztecs (San Diego, CA)
- Southern Illinois Salukis (Carbondale, IL)
- St. Louis University Billikens (St. Louis, MO)
- University of California, Santa Cruz Banana Slugs
- University of California, Irvine Anteaters
- University of New Mexico Lobos (Albuquerque, NM)

The Tools, Repairs, *&* Woodworking *Checklist*

Measure twice, cut once.

Dads are expected to know the basics of home repair, like how to patch drywall. If we can build something out of wood or even just understand "The New Yankee Workshop," our powers to transform raw lumber appear great. Being able to pass along woodworking skills to your children allows them to learn useful skills and spend time doing something fun with you.

For tool basics, take a look at the Toolbox Checklist, a list of the key tools you will need. For our wives and girlfriends, you have to understand that men like looking at tools and even pictures of tools in the Sunday circulars (ever wonder why men will spend lots of time just ambling down aisles of hardware stores with that power tool look in their eyes?). As with life, the right tool for the job is important.

The toolbox is a great place to start thinking about repairs. After that, I mix in some repair tips, home workshop ideas, woodworking skills, and projects.

✔ Toolbox

TOOL TIP: To remember which way to turn a screw, think "Lefty Loosey, Righty Tighty." Turn left or counterclockwise to loosen, right or clockwise to tighten.

Think about what you need day to day. Basics that you'll want to throw in the toolbox include screwdrivers and wrenches and simple hand tools. Then you start accumulating power tools and what you need for specialized tasks. Here is what I would put together for a basic set (buying decent quality will pay off in the long run):

☐ **Screwdriver(s).** I'm sure you've found that the tool you need most around the house is a screwdriver. Since you don't always know if the screws are slotted or Phillips head (the one that looks like an **X**), multipurpose screwdrivers with tips you can change are useful, and they often come with two different size heads for each type of screw. Lots of versatility there. Your other option is to get two medium sized screwdrivers, one slotted and one Phillips head. Sears Craftsman and Stanley are good brands for hand tools.

Next Level: As you build your collection, you can invest in a set of different size single use screwdrivers for more torque with the larger screwdrivers and more precision with the smaller ones.

☐ **Crescent Wrenches.** A medium sized crescent wrench, the kind that adjust with the thumb wheel is useful for gripping and turning nuts. Don't use pliers since they don't grip hard enough, will slip, round off the nut, and make it hard to loosen it.

Next Level: Add a couple different sized crescent wrenches or an adjustable wrench. Then add fixed, open-ended wrenches.

☐ **Vise-grip Wrench.** Sometimes you need more gripping power, so a vise-grip wrench gives you that.

Next Level: Buy a socket wrench set.

☐ **16 oz. Hammer.** For all sorts of jobs. Wooden handled are fine. Unless you are going to be framing houses all day, you don't need to spend a lot of money here.

Next Level: Mallet if you'll be doing woodworking or using chisels. Pry bar if you'll be pulling out a lot of nails or pulling apart a lot of wood. Staple gun if you'll be doing a lot of small projects where staples are better than nails (e.g., new screens).

☐ **Tape Measure.** You may already have this for other uses, but a 25 foot tape measure is indispensable for measuring boards, hanging pictures, and seeing if the couch will fit through the door.

Next Level: Combination Square. Steel ruler.

☐ **Electric Drill.** Get a good cordless or a corded drill. You don't need a large voltage cordless drill unless you will be doing a lot of power drilling. Sometimes cordless drills, though, seem to run out of charge when you need them, so a corded drill is a good choice for around the house and provides a lot of drilling power. Some cordless screwdrivers do not provide enough power for serious work. With any drill, get screwdriver bits and some twist bits. Be sure your drill has variable speed and reverse to back screws out. I use a DeWalt for my corded and cordless drills.

TOOL TIP: Affix a white adhesive label on the side of the tape measure to have a handy place to write down measurements. Better yet, pick up a formica sample square and attach it to the side. You can write down measurements in pencil on your new handy surface and just wipe off or erase when done.

Next Level: Corded or cordless drill, whichever you did not get the first time around. Speed changer to change bits quickly. Larger assortment of drill bits. More screwdriver bits.

☐ **Utility Knife.** A utility knife is great for marking wood, cutting paper or vinyl, rounding wood edges like on a tenon, scraping off bits of paint or old adhesive.

Next Level: There isn't one. This is a basic.

☐ **Wood Saw.** A multipurpose saw for small jobs. You can get ripping (cutting with the grain) and cross-cutting saws, but a general purpose saw usually is fine. I really like the Japanese saws. They are easy to use and make nice, clean cuts.

Next Level: A jigsaw makes short work of cutting off small pieces of wood or boards but is not really accurate or well-suited to larger jobs. For that, you would need at least a circular saw. A circular saw is great for cutting plywood, decking, and 2x4s. Once you've graduated and need something for more exact jobs, consider a table saw. The table saw is the centerpiece of a woodworker's workshop. As you begin building furniture, you might look at dovetail saws and other special saws.

☐ **Hacksaw.** If you need to cut metal or plastic, you will need a hacksaw.

Next Level: Different blades for different materials.

TOOL TIP: Predrilling holes for screws helps prevent wood from splitting.

☐ **Pliers.** A pair of adjustable pliers should be in the toolbox.

Next Level: Needle nose pliers. Wire stripper.

☐ **Putty Knives.** Good for applying all sorts of materials, especially spackle.

Next Level: Caulking gun.

☐ **Wood Glue.** 3 in 1 oil, WD 40.

☐ **Sawhorses.** For supporting boards to be cut, elevating work.

Next Level: Workmate, a portable workbench that folds up, can clamp wood and can be used as a sawhorse.

> **REALITY CHECK:** Giving your child his or her "own" set of tools and a small toolbox will make them feel like real workers. A tack hammer and a couple of screwdrivers, and something to measure with is all it takes to keep them busy.

✓ Quick Measurements

Item	Dimensions
Piece of Paper	8 1/2 inches x 11 inches
Dollar Bill	6.14 inches by 2.61 inches or roughly 6 1/8 x 2 9/16. Folded in half long ways for just over 3 inches, and half again for about 1 1/2 inches. Fold other way for rough 1 1/4 inch.
Credit Card	3 3/8 x 2 1/8 inches
Quarter	About 1 inch diameter (0.955")
Penny	3/4 inch diameter
Finger Tip to Elbow	About 18 inches
Foot	About 10–12 inches
Armspan	About 5–6 feet
Thumb to Forefinger	About 6 inches

REPAIR TIP: When fixing anything, take a second to think about what you'll need and what to do. Then break the problem down into steps. If you're patient and think it through, you'll fix it.

✓ How To Fix Things

Cardinal Rules: if you are working on electrical systems, turn off the power at the circuit breaker box. If you are working on plumbing, turn off the water.

To Fix a Running Toilet

☐ Jiggle the handle to make sure that is not the problem. Really.

☐ Lots of times, all you need to do is replace the flapper valve in the toilet tank. In most toilets, these are easy to replace.

☐ Lift the top off the back of the toilet and see what shape and size the flapper valve is. Look for the round black rubber cover that goes up and down when you flush, pulled on a chain or wire. Buy a new one at a hardware store. The new ones often just fit with a couple rubber tabs on either side that attach to plastic pins in the tank.

☐ Turn off the water at the chrome valve leading into the toilet line, and flush the toilet to drain the tank. Unhook the chain on top of the flapper valve. Remove the old flapper valve. Some come off by slipping off the long tube called the refill tube. Others have "ears" that attach to pins.

☐ Install the new flapper valve by pushing down over the refill tube or attaching the ears to the pins. Make sure that the valve is centered over the opening when the valve is closed.

☐ Reattach the chain to the correct length. Turn the water back on, let the tank fill, and check to be sure the flapper valve is working.

To Clear a Stopped Up Drain

☐ For a toilet, use a plunger. Make sure there is enough water to cover the top of the business end of the plunger. Plunge. If that does not work, you have two choices. First, you can buy an auger, a long, thin piece of flexible metal with a device to make it twist by hand, and try to remove the obstruction. Or, second, you can pay for a plumber's house call.

☐ For a sink, see if you can remove the obstruction from the top of the drain. If not, you may need to open the trap under the sink to drain it and pull out whatever is lodged in there.

TOOL TIP: When working on a sink or shower drain, close and cover the drain so that you do not lose any screws or small parts down the drain. Like many lessons, I learned this one the hard way.

To Patch Drywall

☐ Small dents and dings can be fixed by applying spackle with a putty knife and smoothing it over. Once dry, you can sand it smooth and paint over it.

☐ For larger holes, place a piece of metal mesh over the hole. You can buy these precut with adhesive. Then it's just a job of spackling over the mesh until filled and smooth. Again, sand smooth, wait to dry, and paint. There may be a slight bulge in the wall where you have used the mesh and spackle, but usually it is not noticeable, and after a couple months I bet you could not even find exactly where you repaired the wall.

☐ For large holes, you will need to cut a piece of drywall to fit in the opening, once you have squared the opening. You would also need to create backer rods (small pieces of wood that attach inside the wall) for the new drywall to butt up against.

To Stop A Faucet From Dripping

☐ Usually, the dripping is caused by a worn washer. To fix this, turn off the water at the valve under the sink, for both hot and cold water. The following is for two-handled sink faucets.

☐ Turn off the water.

☐ Many handles have covers, often the "C" and "H" covers, which you should pry off carefully and set aside (and not lose like I did).

☐ Under the cover is a screw. Unscrew it. Use an adjustable wrench to loosen the packing nut on top (counterclockwise). Pull out the valve assembly. Inspect the washer and **O**-ring.

☐ Replace a worn washer by unscrewing the retaining screw and taking off the old washer. This may be beveled or flat. If you do not have a replacement on hand, take the washer with you to the hardware store to make sure you match it correctly. Same thing with an **O**-ring.

☐ Replace the old washer and **O**-rings with new ones. Reinstall the valve assembly in reverse order, with packing nut tightened back and handle screwed back on. If the faucet continues to leak, the valve seat may need to be replaced. You can do this with a special seating tool or call a plumber to do it. For one-handled sink faucets, repairing leaks is usually done by replacing the **O**-ring first, and if that does not work replacing the entire mechanism called the cartridge.

✔ Build with Wood – Building Block Skills

Hammering

☐ Grip near the end of the hammer, and let the weight of the hammer help do the work.

☐ For finish work, use a nail protector to save the wood surface from misses. You can buy plastic ones or make one out of thin wood, plastic, or even heavy cardboard. Just make a slit where the nail would be, slide over, and the rest of the object's surface is protected.

□ Use nail sets to finish nailing and protect the wood. Leave the head of the nail 1/16th inch above the wood's surface, and then use the nail set to drive the nail head below the surface.

Hand Sawing

□ Point the index finger along the direction of your handsaw for more control.

□ Start sawing at an angle to make a notch, then continue sawing.

□ Support the work at all times.

□ Remember when measuring to account for the width of the saw blade (kerf). Cut on the waste side of the line if you are cutting off a board. If you are cutting a few lengths out of one board, subtract the ⅛ inch or so that the kerf will make so you do not end up with boards that are too short.

Fasteners

□ You can use drywall screws in woodworking. They hold well, are easy to drive, and are stronger than brass and other soft metals. Screws hold better than nails but are more likely to split the wood unless you pre-drill the hole. Use drywall screws on joints that won't be seen or countersink the hole and fill with wood putty once you've driven the screw.

□ Brass wood screws used for nice finish work are not strong and will break off or strip. Pre-drill holes or screw a drywall screw in first and then back it out and replace it with a brass screw.

TOOL TIP: Nails are measured by pennyweight, abbreviated with a "d." Don't say "4-Dee" nails for 4d. Say "four penny" nails. An 8d is an eight-penny nail. Nails go from the ½ inch 2d to the 6 inch 60d, though most commonly used nails are in the 4d-8d range, 1 ½ inches to 2½ inches. "Common" nails have larger heads and are used for construction. "Finish" nails have small heads and are used for finer work where they can be driven below the surface of the wood.

TOOL TIP: When marking a board for cutting, put an **X** on the waste side to avoid a mistake.

TOOL TIP: To pull nails out of wood, use a wood block under the hammer both for leverage and to avoid marring the wood.

Wood Filler

☐ To fill a small hole in wood, use wood putty, let it dry, and sand it smooth. You can fill a larger hole with a golf tee or small dowel coated with wood glue and hammered into the hole. Let the tee or dowel dry and then saw off the excess and sand smooth.

Sanding

☐ Sanding is boring but necessary to finish any wood project. Sand with the grain, except when you use a random orbit sander. For flat pieces that you are hand sanding, wrap the sandpaper around a wood block to get a better finish and increase the life of the sandpaper. Use a sanding sponge for irregular shapes or surfaces. If you are sanding near where wood grains run perpendicular to each other, cover the other side with some cardboard or masking tape near the edge.

Sandpaper Grades and Uses

Grit	Description and Uses
50–60	Very Coarse. Rare for woodworking. Used to remove paint or even out gouged wood. This grade tears up wood and is hard to correct.
80–100	Coarse. This is the lowest grit you might use for sanding projects where there are noticeable defects that need to be smoothed out.
120–180	Medium. This is the grit you most often use to start finishing most wood projects.
220–280	Fine. Finish sanding.
320–400	Very Fine. For between certain finish coats and wet sanding.

TOOL TIP: For sawing plywood, use masking tape to cover where your cut will be and draw your cut line over the tape. The tape helps prevent splintering and tearout.

TOOL TIP: When building, check for square by measuring the diagonals. If you build a tabletop, measure from corner to opposite corner diagonally. If the two diagonals are equal, the tabletop is square.

TOOL TIP: Drill straight using a try square or a square wood block to guide you. Make sure the drill bit is lined up parallel with the square or block.

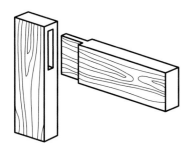

Mortise and Tenon

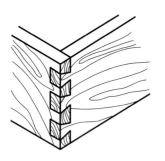

Dovetail Joint

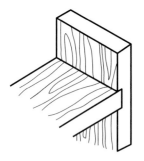

Dado Joint

Wood Dimensions

☐ Lumber has nominal sizes but once "dressed," or milled smooth, the real measurements are less than listed. A 2 x 4 is not 2 inches by 4 inches. It's a half inch less on each side. Just as a 2 x 4 is really 1½ x 3½, a 4 x 4 is really 3½ x 3½. This is for softwoods like pine. The sizes of sheet goods like plywood are, however, what their measurements say they are. A full four foot by eight foot plywood board is 4 x 8 (a lot of wood to carry, and at ¾ inch thick, heavy). If you need plywood, unless you need the full sheet uncut, get the lumberyard to cut it in half so it will be easier to handle (and fit in your car).

Wood Joints

☐ Butt joints are the weakest, where you butt one piece of wood against the other and glue, nail, or screw it together. You would need to support a butt joint with a brace or wooden ovals called biscuits inserted in slots cut with a biscuit joiner machine.

☐ There are stronger joints for wood projects. Mortise and tenon joints, for example, are often used to attach sides of a table, or aprons, to the legs. They will hold with just glue after being clamped up, though they are sometimes pinned with dowels. Tight-fitting dovetails are also used for finer furniture projects, especially for attaching drawer fronts to the sides. They can be hand cut or made using a router and dovetailing jig.

☐ Dado joints are used in making furniture with shelves, where the groove supports the shelf side.

☐ Rabbets are like half dados, a slot on an open end for a piece of wood to fit into. On a bookcase, for example, the back part of the sides will have a rabbet milled out to accept a plywood back so that the back sits flush with the sides.

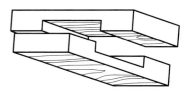

Half Lap Joint

☐ Lap joints are used less often, but I like the way they look. Half lap joints, for example, are made by cutting half the thickness from matching pieces so that when put together they fit into the opposing slots. Bridle joints are kind of a cross between tenons and lap joints, where one piece has a tenon in the middle and the other has a slot in the top to accept the tenon. The slot is not hidden as it might be in a mortised joint. Tongue and groove joints are used for long pieces, as with the back of a bookcase or entertainment center or the sides of a blanket chest.

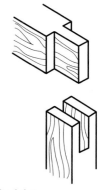

Bridle Joint

☐ Miter joints are made by angling the cuts in the ends of wood pieces. You can cut 45 degree angles in two pieces to create a 90 degree angle as with a mirror frame or face frame around a bookcase.

☐ Dowels and biscuits are methods of attaching wood pieces without cutting difficult joints. Splines are thin wood strips inserted into hidden grooves in joints, to help fasten the joints together. Biscuits, small oval pieces of wood, often replace splines because the special tool that can cut the slots for the manufactured biscuits, the biscuit joiner, is so easy to use.

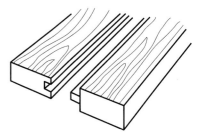

Tongue and Groove

✔Key Power Tools and Accessories for the Home Workshop

Safety Equipment

☐ Buy and use safety glasses or goggles at all times, even if you are making "just one cut." Safety glasses are useless in a drawer or on the shelf. I teach my children that you always have to wear them. It could be that one time you decide you are making just one quick cut that the accident happens. I leave my safety glasses on my table saw so that I see them and cannot cut anything without having to pick them up.

☐ "Think Safety" all the time and set a good example. Stop when you're tired or if you are not comfortable making that last table saw cut. This will also keep you from making a mistake and mis-cutting the piece of wood.

☐ Along with safety glasses, get some ear protection. While you may not need it all the time, you will really want it when running a router for example. A dust mask or respirator should be part of your shop for when you need them. Wood dust can cause respiratory problems, severe ones depending on the type of wood. I bet a lot of us who work in our garages don't have dust collection systems though. If you are making adjustments to a power tool, unplug it. If you are leaving your shop, unplug the tools so that children cannot start them up.

> **REALITY CHECK:** Make sure your children have their own safety glasses. Even though you may not allow them to be nearby when using power tools, it's a good example for them. They'll probably wear them even when not in the workshop.

Table Saw

☐ The table saw is the epicenter of the workshop. The basic saw should include a guard. It should be heavy enough to be stable and durable. The rip fence should be easy to adjust. Next to safety, the most important thing about the table saw is to set it up properly so that cuts are square. Delta is top of the line, but I have been using my Sears Craftsman for years without a problem.

☐ Table Saw Accessories. Safety equipment (in addition to installed guard): Tools to push the wood through without endangering your hands, including push sticks, push blocks, zero clearance inserts.

☐ Blades. Combination blade for ripping (cutting with grain) and crosscutting. If you are a weekend woodworker, it's not worth the time to change between a dedicated ripping blade and dedicated crosscutting blade unless you are going to be doing a lot of either one at any one time. You will soon want a dado cutter, either the less expensive and perfectly adequate wobble type or the better quality stacked dado head cutter. Unplug the saw when you are changing blades.

☐ Measuring. While the tape measure and metal ruler are useful, you may want to get a height gauge to check blade height. You can also use measured wood blocks to check height.

☐ Support. Outfeed rollers or extension tables to support wood running over the edge of the table.

Router

☐ Once you start getting into woodworking, you will find that you want a router to mill wood. You can create interesting edges and joints with a router and router table. Buy a router with a motor powerful enough for what you plan to do. Porter-Cable makes a good router. You will also want to pick up a selection of bits: straight, rabbeting, beading, round over, and chamfer. Though you will pay more initially, carbide tipped bits will last longer and cut better over time than high-speed steel bits. If you will be doing a lot of milling or cutting mortises and tenons, buy or make a router table.

Clamps

☐ You can never have too many clamps. **C**-clamps are less useful for woodworking, and you need to take care not to mar the wood so use wood blocks to protect the surface. Bar clamps are more useful, and the best (and most expensive) bar clamps are the squeeze grip types. You wouldn't want to spend all your tool money on them but a set or two will be mighty helpful. If you plan to create large pieces like table tops you will want some pipe clamps. When you use pipe clamps, use wood scraps between the clamp and the pieces you are gluing up. Scrap dowels work, too, on edges to protect the wood and to distribute the clamping pressure. Be careful with pipe clamps because they can really apply a lot of force, much more than you need for gluing up boards where you risk squeezing out too much glue and deflecting the boards. Spring clamps from Pony are useful for holding smaller pieces together. For irregular shaped items, you will want a band clamp (strap).

Electrical Cord

☐ Of course you need this before the power tools, but get one that is properly rated for the load and distance.

Glue

☐ Yellow wood glue is the basic. It holds well when properly applied, clamped, and cured. Elmer's and Tite-Bond are two brands. You may need waterproof glue for some projects.

> **REALITY CHECK:** One of my sons enjoys the workshop when he can glue. He has his own small bottle of wood glue and access to a bucket of wood scraps. He makes toys, buildings, airplanes, and swords out of the scraps. It's a great introduction to woodworking.

Measuring

☐ Tape measure, metal ruler, metal straight edge with clamps, combination square.

Sanders

☐ Take a look at a belt sander and random orbit sander. Later on you may want a palm sander for finish work. A belt sander is great for boards and edges, but it can take off a lot of wood in a short time and round over edges if you are not careful. I tend to use the random orbit sander most on furniture projects and finish up with hand sanding.

Band Saw

☐ A lot of pros swear by the band saw, even over the table saw. They're multipurpose, can rip and crosscut, make fine cuts, and are a workhorse – if you get a big, heavy duty bandsaw. The small ones with little wood capacity are useful but not as versatile. Bandsaws also take a lot of care and feeding to get them adjusted just right. I personally would go for the table saw first, but a good bandsaw would be high on the wishlist.

Biscuit Joiner

☐ This tool is relatively new to the weekend woodworker toolbox, but it is incredibly useful for making sure glued up tabletops are even and joints strong. I might've moved this up on the priority list depending on what kind of projects I was planning.

Planer

☐ A stationary thickness planer is a luxury. Still, if I had one I wouldn't complain. You can also buy a handheld planer, which is most useful for planing down edges but can also be use to help flatten boards. A power planer can substitute for a jointer, which is an expensive and fairly limited purpose tool (in fairness, pros would call it a necessity) for squaring board edges.

Drill Press

☐ This can be a useful tool, again depending on what you plan to build.

Mortiser

☐ Another nice tool but expensive for a single purpose tool.

Miter Saw

☐ A power miter saw or chop box is great if you are cutting a lot of molding or making angle and crosscuts. In most cases, your table saw can handle these cuts, though, if you don't want to spend the money.

Lathe

☐ Some people like to turn their own table legs or make bowls. Need a lathe to do that.

Air Compressor and Nail Gun

☐ This would be nice to have, but unless you're doing a lot of nailing, a hammer works fine.

Radial Arm Saw

☐ I don't see a need for a big overhead radial arm saw that is really useful only for crosscutting and to me is not as safe as a table saw. Better off saving your money.

Grinder

☐ Many home-based woodworkers have grinders to help maintain the sharp edges on their tools. You can do a lot with sharpening stones, though, without the electric powered tools. A diamond stone like those from DMT handles many sharpening tasks in the workshop.

Hand Tools

☐ In addition to the ones in your toolbox already, you would want to add a plane, wood chisels and mallet, an awl, a straight edge, marking knife (or replace the blade on your utility knife), files, rasps, and nail sets.

✓ Projects to Build with Your Children

With any of these projects, depending on the age of your children, you might want to cut the wood in advance. Also, explain to the kids before you get started what you are going to build together and maybe sketch it out. Remember, the fun part is the hammering and painting, not the sanding. Be safe – use safety glasses or goggles.

Small Toolbox for Children

This is a nice project to work on together, and it gives your child a place to keep a few tools so that when he's building with you he can have his own set.

☐ You'll use ½ inch plywood for the bottom and sides, and a ¾ inch diameter dowel for the handle. Half inch plywood is lighter and less expensive than ¾ inch plywood, though you could substitute pine or ¾ inch plywood for this project if you adjust the measurements. Also, when assembling, ½ inch plywood gives you less of an edge to nail into so be careful there. You'll also need some 1¼" screws or nails.

☐ Cut pieces as follows:
(1×) Bottom piece 12" × 6"
(2×) Long sides 13" × 4"
(2×) Ends 6½" × 6"
(1×) Handle 13" dowel (¾" diameter)

☐ Drill a ¾" hole near the tops of the end pieces (about 1½" down). You'll need a ¾" bit (spade bit). If the hole is not big enough, run the drill bit around the edges of the hole. Leave enough room at the top so that there is plenty of wood to support the handle when holding the box. Next, trim the top two corners off each end so that you have a 45 degree angle on each side of the top of the ends.

☐ Attach the end pieces to the bottom with yellow (carpenter's) glue and two nails or two screws (predrill the holes for the screws to avoid splitting the wood). The nails or screws will pull the joint tight while the glue sets.

☐ Attach the sides the same way, with glue on the edges and a few screws or nails to secure the sides to the ends and the bottom. You don't need tons of screws or nails since the glue will form a strong bond. Glue the dowel in place by putting some glue on each end and sliding back in place. Sand the box with 150 grit sandpaper. Your child can paint the box if he or she wishes. You should have your child sign and date each project.

Toy Boat

This is a good, simple project if you have scrap pine boards around. Cut the base of the boat out of pine, maybe 8 inches long and 4 inches wide. Trim the front corners so that the block of wood looks "boat" shaped with a bow.

☐ Have your child sand the base/keel and some small wood blocks. Glue on the wood blocks to build up the decks. Dowels make good smokestacks. The most fun part – after gluing – is painting it!

What We've Built

☐ _____

☐ _____

☐ _____

☐ _____

☐ _____

Bookends

This project is simple but gives your child something he can build with you and give as a gift.

☐ Cut four 6" × 6" boards out of ¾" pine, or, if you want to upgrade, poplar. Do not use plywood. If you want to get fancy, use a jigsaw to cut an arch shape at the top of the two pieces that will be the upright pieces.

☐ Predrill and countersink holes through the bottom part of the top piece where it would go into the base piece. You can avoid this step if you plan to use nails. Sand the pieces before assembly, using 150 grit sandpaper.

☐ Glue the top piece to the base piece, and attach with screws or nails. Finish sand with 220 grit sandpaper. Again, the best part is that your child can decorate it however he or she wants, with paint, drawing, gluing pieces onto it, placing an interesting rock on the base.

TOOL TIP: It is easier if you sand parts of any wood project before assembling because then you don't have to worry about getting in the edges.

The Cars & Boats *Checklist*

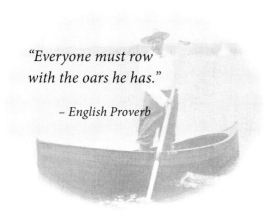

"Everyone must row with the oars he has."

– English Proverb

A basic familiarity with what goes on under the hood is one of those areas fathers are supposed to know about, even though auto mechanics now rely heavily on computer diagnostics.

Knowing how to change a flat, jump a dead battery, and check the oil, though, are the basic skills we are expected to have. Boats, too, are something we should know a little about, so I've added some small craft basics.

 Cars

Three car maintenance and repair basics.

☐ Changing a Flat

1. Safety first. Make sure the car is on level ground, in Park (or in gear if a manual), with the emergency brake on. If you have a block for the tires, that would be a good safety measure. Make sure you are well off the road, put on your emergency flashers, and if you have a reflector or flare use that to warn other drivers. If you cannot change the tire in safety, wait for help.

2. Get the equipment out (this assumes you have the spare, jack, and tire iron/lug nut wrench). Read the instructions that come with them. Many car manufacturers now have pasted-on diagrams or cards that illustrate the steps.

3. Take off the hubcap. You may need the the tire iron to pry it off.

4. Next, loosen the lug nuts, working across in a star pattern. Do not jack up the car yet. Loosen each nut a little bit at a time at the start instead of taking one entirely off and moving on to the next one. This makes sure that there is more even pressure on each one. Do not completely unscrew the lug nuts yet.

5. Read the instructions on the jack about where to place it under the car and how to use it. Follow the instructions and jack the car up, only enough so that you'll be able to remove the tire. The tire can still touch the ground lightly.

6. Remove all of the lug nuts. To keep from losing them, put them in the upturned hubcap, away from where you'll kick it over.

7. Pull the old tire off the bolts.

8. Put the new tire up on the bolts. Put the lug nuts on, tighten them down by hand as far as you can. Then, using the tire iron, tighten each one in turn working around in that same star pattern you used to loosen them, tightening each one a bit as you go around until you have gone all around and they are all tight.

9. Lower the car. Recheck the lug nuts to make sure that they are tight. Replace the hubcap. Store the flat tire, jack, and tire iron. Get on your way again. Be sure to get the flat repaired.

☐ Checking the Oil

1. In most cars, this is pretty simple. Look for a dipstick marked "Oil." Pull the dipstick and wipe it off with a paper towel.

2. Reinsert it, and pull it out again. You should see the oil level near the end of the metal, which is marked with a legend like "Add" or "Safe." The oil should be light brown and not cloudy.

☐ Jump Starting a Car Battery

1. First things first. (1) Carry good quality 15 foot jumper cables with you. (2) Be careful. Batteries contain acid – make sure

> **CAR TIP:** Lug nuts are often installed using an air driven impact wrench. They are hard to loosen. One way to do it is to put a piece of pipe over the end of the lug wrench. This gives you a longer lever to help in freeing the lug nuts. Or, you can buy one of those four way tire irons, which will also give you some more leverage than the small ones auto manufacturers provide.

the battery you are trying to power is not visibly damaged and is not frozen. Don't put your face over it. (3) Call or flag down a friend or someone who looks normal to help you jumpstart your car.

2. Place the two cars where the jumper cables can reach, but the cars should not touch. Turn off both cars.

3. Attach one RED cable to the DEAD battery's POSITIVE (+) terminal.

4. Attach the other end of the same RED cable to the POSITIVE (+) terminal of the GOOD (booster) battery.

5. Attach one end of the other cable, the BLACK cable, to the NEGATIVE (-) terminal of the good battery.

6. Attach the other end of that BLACK cable to the engine block or unpainted metal part of the car with the dead battery but attach AWAY from the dead battery. Do NOT attach the negative cable to the dead battery.

7. Stand back. Start the car that has the good battery. Let it run, then start the car with the dead battery.

8. Once running, disconnect the cables in the reverse order from how you attached them. (Leave the car with the once-dead battery still running – don't turn it off and let that hard work go to waste. The battery will need some running time to charge up.)

☐ Clutch Stuff

Diesel vs. Gasoline. The main difference between diesel and gas engines besides the fuel they take is that gas engines use spark plugs to ignite the gas/air mixture in the cylinder while diesel engines do not use spark plugs, instead injecting the diesel fuel into the cylinder with air that has been compressed. The compression creates heat so that the diesel fuel combusts. Diesel engines are more efficient.

Why You Should Refill Often. If you're like my family, I like to fill up the car when it gets down to around a half tank while my wife likes to wait until we're running on fumes. Here's support for filling up early. A nearly empty tank allows water vapor to build up more in the gas tank and allows more of the sediment from the bottom of the tank to go into the fuel line, neither of which is great for the engine, though there is a fuel filter to help clean the gas feeding into the engine.

Oil. You put in the oil that the manufacturer recommends but what does that mean? The viscosity rating like 10W-30 or 10W-40 measures the oil's thickness or how well it flows. Too high viscosity may not allow the oil to flow where it needs to. Too low viscosity may not adequately protect the engine. The "W" means the oil is acceptable for winter use. Nowadays, motor oils work well in a wide range of different temperatures.

Octane. The octane rating measures how much the gasoline can be compressed in the car's cylinder before there is "knocking" or spontaneous combustion. Low octane gas knocks at a lower compression than high octane fuel.

Fours. Four on the floor is a four speed manual shift located on the floor and not on the steering column. 4x4 is four wheel drive. 4x2 is two wheel drive.

☐ Standard Transmission

Driving a standard is cool. Here's what you need to handle a manual.

Some Basics. The clutch is on the far left. Pressing down on it disengages the gears. Letting it out engages the gears. The gearshift usually has an **H** pattern with neutral in the center, and four (or five) speeds plus reverse.

Play with shifting the gears, with the car off. Have your good friend, the manual transmission car owner (like my friend since second grade David), demonstrate since it is his car. Push the clutch in, put the car in first, and let the clutch out gently. Try progressing up through the gears.

Later, when you're driving, you'll be able to tell a lot from the sound of the gears. A grinding sound means that the car is not in gear. Push on the clutch, shift fully into gear, and ease the clutch back out. A laboring sound, or a chugging, means you're in third, say, when you should be in second. At the other end, if you have a high pitched whirring or revving sound, you should shift up to a higher gear. Don't "ride the clutch." What that means is to avoid wearing it down, you should not keep the clutch pressed in more than you need to. For example, if you're going to be at a stop for a while, put the car in neutral instead of holding the clutch down for a long time.

To start, put the car in neutral. If you don't the car jumps forward when you try to start it. Do not press the clutch yet. Some people like to park with their cars in first, so in that case press the clutch in and start the car.

To get started, car is running, clutch is in, gear is shifted into first. Now, ease out the clutch. (It's good to practice all this in a level and empty parking lot.) When the clutch starts to engage the gear, the car should begin to move forward. Just at that point, you can give the car some gas. Basically, as you practice, you will feel the clutch coming up while the gas pedal goes down, smoothly synchronized to get the car in the right gear. Sometimes you will let the clutch out too quickly ("pop the clutch") and the car will jump forward or stall. With practice that will happen less.

That's the basic maneuver, repeated for the other gears. So, when you successfully get the car into first gear, you can let off the gas, push in the clutch, shift to second, let the clutch out slowly while giving the car some gas. Once you've practiced this in the empty parking lot, you can move on (under the car owner's supervision) to 3rd and 4th gears, eventually becoming able to start the car going uphill. You should also watch your friend and learn to use reverse and to downshift using descending gears to slow down.

☐ Car Stuff That You Need

1. In addition to the AAA card and cellphone you carry for emergencies, your glove compartment should contain:

☐ Vehicle registration
☐ Owner's manual
☐ Maps
☐ Small flashlight
☐ Handi wipes and kleenex, pens and paper
☐ Swiss Army knife or Leatherman multipurpose tool
☐ Tire pressure gauge
☐ Insurance info

2. Trunk or storage container should have these key emergency items:

☐ Tire change equipment (inflated spare; jack; tire iron/lug nut wrench).
☐ Flashlight with good batteries, not those old corroded ones you left for two years under the seat. You could try to replace batteries when you replace smoke detector batteries, every daylight savings time shift.
☐ Reflectors or flares.
☐ Jumper cables.
☐ Tools if you can use them (pocketknife, flat and Phillips head screwdrivers, wrench, pliers).
☐ Gloves, cap, bandannas.

- [ ] Blanket. Those emergency mylar blankets are useful and don't take up much space.
- [ ] In winter, you may want to toss in a shovel and some sand.
- [ ] A couple bottles of water for emergencies (for drinking or radiator).
- [ ] Basic First Aid kit.
- [ ] Some people carry engine fluids like oil and antifreeze. If you are going to be places you can't get them, go ahead. Otherwise, I'd say save the space.

[ ] Some of the Best Cars of All Time

Best: (in no particular order except #1)
- Your first
- Jaguar E-Type, 1961–1975
- Chevrolet Corvette Stingray, 1963 or 1957
- Ferrari 250 GTO, 1962
- Porsche 911, 1961 on
- Ford Mustang, especially 1965 Shelby GT 350
- Mercedes Benz 300SL gullwing, 1956

Worst:
- Ford Pinto, Yugo, AMC Pacer

 # Boats

Boys read the Hornblower series and graduate to Patrick O'Brian's Aubrey-Maturin series of sea stories. We romanticize the sea and respect the power of the waves, and we recall the prayer "O God, the sea is so great, and my boat is so small." We learn from our grandfathers how to fish, as I did on the York River in Virginia and my sons did at the Deanna Rose Children's Farmstead pond in Kansas.

Ships at a distance have every man's wish on board.

– Zora Neale Hurston

The first rule of the sea for small craft is to carry enough life jackets, also known as personal flotation devices or PFDs, for everyone and have everyone – especially children – wear them. PFDs need to meet Coast Guard requirements, and they need to fit. If you are going to be doing a lot of boating on heavily traveled waterways, take a boating safety class.

☐ Rules of the "Road" for Boats

Take a boating course to understand the navigation rules. Stay clear of large ships and barges. They don't stop quickly, a lot of times can't see you in a small boat, and even if you technically have the right of way you will lose every time. There are clear navigational rules for boaters that set out who has the so-called privilege when boats meet, but the main rule is that the captain must avoid collision.

☐ Small Boat Stuff You Need

For small craft, you should carry the following (check also with the Coast Guard):

☐ Boat registration
☐ Owner's manual
☐ Navigation rules
☐ PFDs for each person
☐ Throwable PFD
☐ Required safety devices, depending on boat size, like fire extinguishers, visual distress signaling device, air horn or sound warning device
☐ Radio and/or cell phone
☐ Anchor, extra line
☐ Bailer
☐ Charts, compass and/or GPS system
☐ Tools, multi-purpose tool, and spare parts
☐ Paddle
☐ Flashlight
☐ Sunscreen
☐ Drinking water
☐ Binoculars
☐ First Aid kit

> *For the truth is that I already know as much about my fate as I need to know. The day will come when I will die. So the only matter of consequence before me is what I will do with my allotted time. I can remain on shore, paralyzed with fear, or I can raise my sails and dip and soar in the breeze.*
>
> — *Richard Bode,* First You Have to Row a Little Boat

☐ Main Running Lights

- Red on Port (left). (Port wine is red.)
  (Port = Left. Remember "port" and "left" each have four letters.)
- Green on starboard (right).
- White on stern.
- Plus white masthead light on larger powerboats and on some
  sailboats.

Other light combinations show what the boat is doing. For example, red over white signals a fishing boat. White over white over white is for a tug towing a long tow (over 200 meters). At night, if you see a boat's red, green, and white lights, you are meeting the boat head on. If you see only the white light, you are approaching the boat from its stern (or the boat is anchored or it is a sailboat).

☐ Nautical Terms

- Port is left.
- Starboard is right.
- Aft is behind or back toward the stern.
- Forward is toward the bow.
- The galley is the kitchen.
- The head is the toilet.

If you read books about old sailing ships, you'll know that the area around a boat is divided into a 32 point circle. So when the captain tells the helmsman to steer up a point, it means change direction 11.25 degrees into the wind. "Abeam" is at 90 degrees and 270 degrees. The points of the compass were later designated more specifically by degrees. Earlier than that, in early maps, you can see the names for directions, after winds like the levante in the east, sirocco in the southeast, tramontana in the north, and maestro in the northwest.

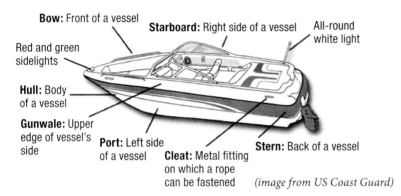

Bow: Front of a vessel
Starboard: Right side of a vessel
All-round white light
Red and green sidelights
Hull: Body of a vessel
Gunwale: Upper edge of vessel's side
Port: Left side of a vessel
Cleat: Metal fitting on which a rope can be fastened
Stern: Back of a vessel
(image from US Coast Guard)

"Close-hauled" means sailing as nearly as the boat can into the wind, usually around 45 degrees. Sailboats that try to sail directly into the wind lose steerage way and are said to be "in irons," which is why sailboats "tack" at angles to the wind to sail in the general direction of where the wind is coming from. As a sailboat sails away from the wind, it goes from "close reach" to "beam reach" (about 90 degrees off the wind), to "broad reach" to "running" directly opposite the wind direction.

On old sailing ships, especially when few sailors had watches, bells were used to keep time. Sailors kept "watch," however, at four hour stretches, with two, two hour watches called "Dog Watches" to make sure that watches alternated each day and gave each watch or set of sailors time to eat dinner in the evening. Within each watch, bells would ring on the half hour, up to eight bells when four hours into the watch.

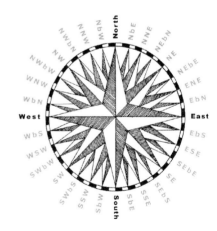

The little "b" above stands for "by" as in north by east.

☐ Watch Periods

Watch	Time
Middle or Graveyard Watch	Midnight to 4 am
Morning Watch	4 am to 8 am
Forenoon Watch	8 am to noon
Afternoon Watch	Noon to 4 pm
First Dog Watch	4 pm to 6 pm
Second Dog Watch	6 pm to 8 pm
First Watch	8 pm to midnight

☐ Boating Tips

Remember, as my grandfather and father taught me on the York River, "Red Right Return." When returning to port, keep the red buoys on your right or starboard side; outbound boats keep green buoys to the right.

The One-Third Rule: For powerboats, use 1/3 of your fuel to go out and 1/3 to return. Keep 1/3 in reserve for emergencies.

For large waves or wakes, turn the bow to take it at an angle.

☐ Tying to a Boat Cleat

Let's say you get invited sailing one day, and the captain asks you to fasten a line to a cleat. Don't pile on figure eight after figure eight. Fasten it like you have spent two years before the mast: Take the line around the base of the cleat, up over the top, back down and around (under) the end, back over the top, down around the other end, and when you come back up around, bring the free end under the working end (they will go side by side the same direction), which will pull down on the line and keep it from slipping.

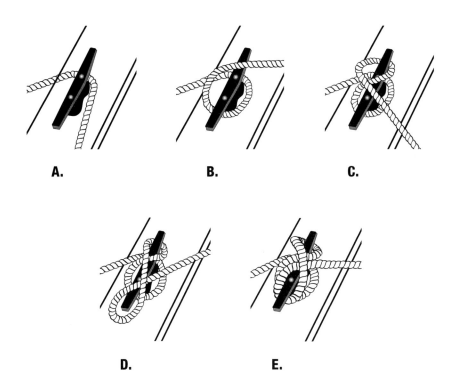

A.   B.   C.

D.   E.

☐ Name Your Boat

If you ever get a boat of your own, from a canoe to a powerboat, think about having a ceremony to name it. You can recite the prayer about your boat being small, or one of following:

They that go down to the sea in ships,
That do business in great waters –
These saw the works of the Lord,
And His wonders in the deep.

—*Psalm 107: 23–24*

○

I must down to the seas again,
to the lonely sea and the sky,
And all I ask is a tall ship
and a star to steer her by.

—*John Masefield*

☐ Signal Flags

Flag	Name	Flag	Name
	Alfa		November
	Bravo		Oscar
	Charlie		Papa
	Delta		Quebec
	Echo		Romeo
	Foxtrot		Sierra
	Golf		Tango
	Hotel		Uniform
	India		Victor
	Juliet		Whiskey
	Kilo		Xray
	Lima		Yankee
	Mike		Zulu

☐ Weather Pennants

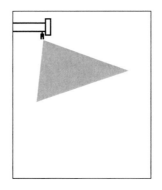

Small Craft Warning:
Winds up to 38 mph

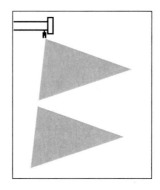

Gale Warning:
Winds up to 54 mph

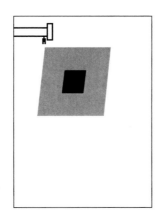

Storm Warning:
Winds 55–73 mph

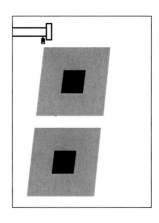

Hurricane Warning:
Winds 74+ mph

The Grilling *&* Home Cooking *Checklist*

Give a man a fish, feed him for a day. Teach a man to fish, feed him for life.

What do you cook when you're alone with the kids, can't think of anything they'll eat, and were instructed "No Taco Bell"? If you want to try a home-cooked meal, to impress the wife when she gets back and to get the children to eat something, here are some ideas beyond chips, Cheerios, and chunky peanut butter.

First thing to remember. Dads own the grill. Anything that has to be charred outdoors, that's our job. We have big tools for grilling and lots of flame that we're not afraid to use. (The use of actual flame makes it is acceptable to say "marinade.")

After grilling basics, we move on to some quick in-the-kitchen meals and snacks. I'm saving the bartending tips and drinks for another time.

✔ Grilling

(I'm not going to insult you by going into grilling safety. Don't sue me if you singe your eyebrows by squirting lighter fluid on the grill.) Let's get cookin'.

What you need for charcoal grilling:

- ☐ Grill
- ☐ Charcoal
- ☐ Optional – "chimney" and some old newspaper
- ☐ Lighter
- ☐ Grill cleaning brush
- ☐ Mesh grill for fish
- ☐ Long-handled tongs, spatula, and fork
- ☐ BBQ sauce brush
- ☐ Knife to cut into meat to check for doneness
- ☐ Optional – Mitts
- ☐ Can of beer

Fire It Up

You can mound some quick start charcoal on the charcoal grate of the grill or put the charcoal in a "chimney," one of those metal canisters that funnels the heat and flame up. I used to use the metal chimney but didn't think it worked as well and you can't pile up as many coals. Real men use a trainload more coals than we really need. If you do use the chimney, start it with two or three pieces of loosely wadded up half sheets of newspaper under the chimney, and use a long lighter.

Fire it up. Risky idea to add lighter fluid once the charcoal is lit, and you don't need it all if you use the quick start type of charcoal. Let the charcoal burn until the briquettes are turning gray and then spread them out if you haven't already. I like to leave some charcoal grouped together to create a hot spot where I need more BTUs. If you are using indirect grilling, you will want to create a ring so that the food does not burn on direct heat or flame. Of course, if you use a gas grill, it's much quicker since all you have to do is to fire up the burners and adjust the flame. Something to be said for that when people are hungry.

Clean off the upper (cooking) grill with the grill brush and put the grill on long enough before you are going to cook so that it gets hot. Back to charcoal grilling. Test the heat. Usually, if the charcoal has just turned gray, those coals will be superhot.

I'm more of a "direct method" griller for steaks, chicken, veggies, burgers, dogs and tofu pups (acceptable so long as grilled). This is where you can sear the meat by cooking briefly on both sides to lock in flavor before you leave it on longer to cook through. Direct grilling also requires the food to be turned.

"Indirect" grilling is cooking (obviously) not directly over the flame like for roasts, whole chickens, ribs. Indirect roasts the food usually with the lid on and does not require turning. Some people recommend using the top to trap more heat and speed up the cooking for direct grilling, too. I don't think it makes much difference, and I like to be more hands on with the grilling, flipping, turning, moving the food around. Use a wire brush to clean off the grill before you use it again. Remove ashes from the bottom of the grill.

COOKING TIP: You can test grilling heat by holding your open hand a fist's width above the grill. The amount of time you can hold it there tells you how hot the grill is:

No. of Seconds	Heat
2	High
3	Med.-High
4	Med
5	Med.-Low
6	Low

☑ Extreme Grilling –
A Few Good Recipes

Our Favorite Meals

☐ _____

☐ _____

☐ _____

☐ _____

☐ _____

☐ **Basic Good Burger.** A classic. Take a chunk of raw hamburger meat, smash it into a hamburger patty, throw it on the grill, cook for several minutes, flip, cook for several more minutes (total time about 8–10 minutes or so). Done and delicious.

☐ **Burger Classic II.** Season the hamburger meat with any of the following before cooking: salt, pepper, Worcestershire sauce, seasoned salt, Tabasco, barbeque sauce. You can also mix into the hamburger meat some chopped onions, green peppers, or anything else you want to cook up. When grilling, near the end of the cooking time, melt a slice of cheddar or provolone. Have on hand lettuce, tomato, sliced onion, pickles, relish, ketchup, mustard, barbeque sauce, bacon.

Next up, some easy steak recipes, with a few "marinades and rubs" to try (how 'bout we call them "BBQ sauce" or "spice" instead of "marinades" and "rubs")

☐ **Basic Naked Steak.** Get a nice cut of meat. Flank steak is usually good but sirloin tips are really good. Fire up the grill. Sear the meat to lock in the flavor. Grill about 10–12 or more minutes a side, depending on how thick it is, until done. Keep an eye on it. When I cut in to test the meat, and I prefer it well done, I like to see almost no pink. Serve with salad and baked potato or potato salad.

☐ **Asian Flank Steak.** Marinate flank steak (see sidebar) in refrigerator a couple hours. Grill about 20 minutes or so, turning halfway, or until done. Slice thin.

☐ **Beef Skewers.** Cube beef or use cubed stew meat and marinate in Beef Skewer Marinade in refrigerator for 1–2 hours. Soak wooden skewers in water during that time. After two hours, put beef on the skewers. Leave space in between the beef cubes. Grill, turning once, about 12 minutes or until done.

☐ **Steak with Dry Rub and Sauce.** Use the Dry Rub for Steak (American Style) on a good cut of steak. Grill for 8–10 minutes, turning halfway, over high heat. Grill for another 8–10 minutes over medium heat, turning. I prefer steaks well done, so add 3–4 more minutes for better done meat.

☐ **Basic Chicken.** Brush four chicken breasts with some olive oil, sprinkle a little salt and pepper. Grill, turning, about 12 minutes until there is no more pink inside.

Steak Marinade (Asian Style):

1 cup soy sauce

1/4 cup scallions

2 tablespoons ginger

2 tablespoons garlic

If you prefer less salt, use low sodium soy sauce or add 1/2 cup water

Beef Skewers Marinade:

1/4 cup soy sauce

1/3 cup ketchup

1/4 cup water

3 tablespoons dark brown sugar

3 tablespoons lime juice

small onion diced

1 tablespoon peanut oil

1 teaspoon grated (or 1/2 teaspoon powdered) ginger

1 teaspoon grated (or 1/2 teaspoon powdered) garlic. This is really good, and you might not think so with the ketchup, but trust me, it works.

Dry Rub for Steak (American Style):

1 tablespoon kosher salt

1 teaspoon pepper

1 teaspoon dry mustard

2 teaspoons paprika

1/2 teaspoon chili powder or cayenne pepper

2 teaspoons garlic powder

1 tablespoon brown sugar

(McCormick's "Montreal Steak" seasoning is also good.)

☐ **Chicken Strips.** Marinate chicken (use thin sliced chicken breasts) several hours in fridge in mix of ½ cup white wine, ¼ cup soy sauce, 2 tablespoons Dijon mustard, and 2 teaspoons oil. Grill as Basic Chicken. Slice into strips.

☐ **Grilled Chicken Tacos.** Season some chicken (use sliced breasts), with salt, pepper, a little powdered garlic, oregano, and a couple teaspoons oil. Grill the chicken 8–10 minutes, turning halfway, until the chicken is firm and no longer pink inside. When you get near the end, warm some tortillas on the grill. Once the chicken is done, cut it into strips or dice it up, wrap it in the tortillas with some guacamole, shredded cheese, and diced tomato, some salsa, and shredded lettuce.

☐ **Basic Fish.** Brush a piece of fresh fish with olive oil. I like swordfish steaks, salmon, tuna steaks, but you can use halibut, trout, bass, mackerel, cod, or whatever you like. Season, if you want, with mild spices (unless you are going for Cajun-style blackened fish), or leave plain. Use a wire mesh fish basket if you have one for flaky fish. Cook both sides, turning, until done.

☐ **Pepper Salmon or Tuna.** Marinate salmon fillets or tuna steaks in soy sauce in fridge for up to an hour. Remove, spray some oil on fillets or steaks, then sprinkle on black pepper. Grill until thoroughly cooked.

✓ Essential Spices

Dads can't go wrong with spices on the hot side. We're ok cooking with pepper. We really don't use thyme or rosemary.

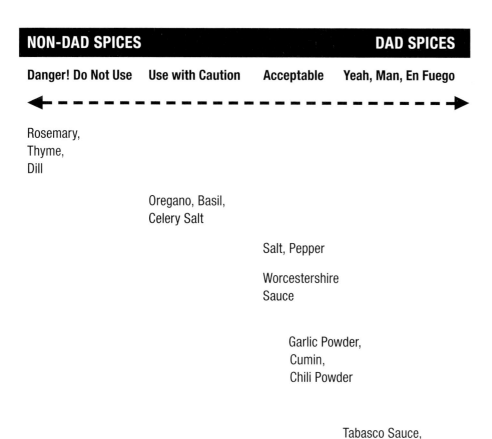

NON-DAD SPICES			DAD SPICES
Danger! Do Not Use	**Use with Caution**	**Acceptable**	**Yeah, Man, En Fuego**

Rosemary,
Thyme,
Dill

Oregano, Basil,
Celery Salt

Salt, Pepper

Worcestershire
Sauce

Garlic Powder,
Cumin,
Chili Powder

Tabasco Sauce,
Cayenne Pepper

✓ Extreme Home Cooking–Dinner Recipes

☐ **Chili Starter Kit**

1. Pour enough vegetable oil to just cover the bottom of a large pot. Set on the stove on medium high.

2. Toss in 1–2 pounds stew meat that's been cut into small pieces. If you like, add 1–2 pounds ground beef. Stir and brown the meat.

3. Once the meat starts to brown, add 2–3 onions chopped up, some salt and pepper. Brown all the way. Drain off the extra oil. Put back on stove.

4. Now, pour in 2 cans red kidney beans, 2 cans dark kidney beans, 1 can tomato paste, and 3 cans tomato sauce.

5. Then, throw in some chopped up green pepper or chili peppers, depending on how hot you want it.

6. Let come to a boil with the lid on.

7. Remove lid, simmer for an hour.

8. Add seasoning – chili powder, a little salt, pepper, maybe a bit of cumin, plus your own secret ingredients (can include beer).

9. Simmer for another couple hours.

10. Serve with cornbread and grated cheddar.

REALITY CHECK: Not all kids like chili. You may want to dial down the spices for children and also try a vegetarian version.

☐ Stew

1. Pour enough vegetable oil to just cover the bottom of a large pot. Set on the stove on medium high.

2. Toss in 1–2 pounds stew meat that's been cut into small pieces. Stir and brown the meat.

3. Once the meat starts to brown, add 2 onions chopped up, some salt and pepper. Brown all the way. Drain off the extra oil. Put back on stove.

4. Add water until the pot is about ¾ full. Cover with lid and let boil.

5. Once boiling, add sliced carrots first to give them a head start as they take longer to cook.

6. After a few minutes, add potato slices or cubes, green pepper pieces, onion slices and/or pearl onions, chopped celery.

7. Simmer for an hour.

8. Add onion soup mix, salt, pepper, a little oregano, basil, and cumin.

9. Simmer for another half hour.

☐ Shepherd's Pie

1. Make a bunch of mashed potatoes (you'll need a lot). Use a mix or boil about 6 or more large peeled Russet potatoes until soft (about 20 minutes), drain and mash with a little milk, salt, and pepper.

2. Brown some hamburger meat in a skillet.

3. Cook 2 cans of corn in a pot.

4. Get a large baking dish. Cover the bottom and sides with the mashed potatoes about a ½ inch thick or a little more.

5. Place a layer of meat on top of the bottom layer of mashed potatoes.

6. Put a layer of corn on top of the meat.

7. Cover the meat with the rest of the mashed potatoes.

8. Bake in the oven at 350 degrees for 30–40 minutes. Check to see if done.

EXTRA CREDIT: You can do several layers, after the potato base, alternate meat, corn, potatoes until you cover with a potato top.

☐ **Burritos**

This is an easy recipe for a quick, tasty meal.

1. Heat up some low-fat refried beans in a pot over medium-low heat.

2. Dice up some tomatoes.

3. In a non-stick pan, with the stove set at medium, give a quick shot of cooking spray.

4. Throw on a tortilla – flour or corn.

5. Let it heat for a minute, flip it, then spoon some heated beans onto the tortilla, throw some Monterey Jack cheese on top of the beans, add a few diced tomatoes, and top off with a couple spoons of salsa.

6. Let heat until the cheese melts, fold over the tortilla, heat the other side. Serve.

✓ Sides

☐ **Marinated Cukes and Onion.** This one's from "The Country," Gloucester, Virginia, where my grandparents had a place. Slice up cucumber and onion. Put in a container with a top. Fill with ⅓ vinegar, ⅔ water, black pepper. Let sit overnight in fridge. A cool summer side with bite.

☐ **Baked Potato.** Use a fork to poke some holes in the potato skin. Put potato in microwave-safe dish. Put in microwave. Press button that says "Baked Potato." Remove from microwave. Split open, and fill with butter, sour cream, salt, pepper, Bacos or bacon bits, broccoli, cheese, Tabasco sauce.

☐ **Homemade Fries.** Slice a potato into thin strips or circles. Set a deep frying pan with ¾ inches of canola oil in it to heat up. When the oil is hot (the oil will pop if you flick a drop of water into it), place the potatoes in it so as not to splash. Cook until brown. Lift out with tongs and set on paper towels to blot some of the oil. Season and serve.

# Dessert

You could go with popsicles or ice cream. Here is my (Southern influenced) signature dessert.

☐ **Pecan Pie.** Buy a crust. Preheat oven to 350 degrees. Mix in a bowl 1 cup sugar, 3 eggs, 1 cup light corn syrup, 2 tablespoons butter, 1 teaspoon vanilla extract. Mix in 1¼ cup chopped pecans. Pour into crust. Bake for 55 minutes or so, until a knife comes out clean. Don't forget the whipped cream.

The Science *&* Technology *Checklist*

*The most important thing
is not to stop questioning.*

– Albert Einstein

Dads should be able to answer why the sky is blue, why grass is green, and what is the speed of light. We should also know a few things about how things work and how to do science tricks (like non-popping balloons). To encourage our children's curiosity, let's take a look at the science questions and answers first. Then we'll turn to a few science tricks.

☑ Science Questions and Answers

☐ Why is the sky blue, sun yellow, and sunset red?

Good questions that children are bound to ask. The sky is blue because light rays are scattered in the atmosphere. Particles in the earth's atmosphere like oxygen and nitrogen atoms, water molecules, dust, and soot scatter light waves. (Sometimes light behaves in waves like when you flip one end of a rope or garden hose. Sometimes light acts like particles, without weight or mass, called photons.)

The shorter blue light waves (shorter wavelength, higher frequency) scatter more than longer red light waves because the blue waves hit more particles than the red ones, which tend to go around more of the particles. You see more of the scattered blue light that reaches your eyes from a lot more angles. Violet has an even shorter wavelength than blue, but our eyes are more sensitive to blue.

During the day, the sun looks yellow because the shorter blue and violet wavelength light is scattered away and the other colors mix to appear yellow.

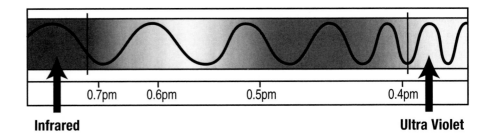

At sunset, when the sun is further away from us, the scattered shorter light waves (violet, blue, and then green) cannot reach our eyes from such distance as much as the longer (red) light waves and we are looking through the earth's atmosphere closer to the earth's surface where there are more particulate pollutants, so we see red sunsets.

☐ Why do we have seasons?

Seasons change because the earth tilts (23.5°) in its orbit around the sun. During summer, part of the earth is tilted closer to the sun so that the sun's rays are more direct on that hemisphere. During winter, the hemisphere is tilted away from the sun so that the light we receive is indirect. The equator is less affected by the tilt, so it stays warm.

☐ Why is grass green?

Grass looks green because it contains chlorophyll, a chemical that plants use to change light into energy to grow (photosynthesis). Chlorophyll reflects green light back to our eyes. Through photosynthesis, grasses, trees, and plants use sunlight to convert water and carbon dioxide found in the air into sugar (glucose) for energy to grow and oxygen, a byproduct. Large forests are able to absorb excess carbon dioxide created by people and give off oxygen. That is why tropical rainforests are so important.

SCIENCE NOTE:
Because light travels so much faster than sound, we see lightning before we hear the thunder. That lets us calculate how far away a thunderstorm is. Start counting when you see the lightning and stop when you hear the thunder. Every five seconds is a mile.

In case you get asked the follow up question, thunder is caused by lightning. Within fractions of a second, lightning heats the air around it to more than 50,000 degrees Fahrenheit, several times hotter than the surface of the sun. The superheated air expands outward at high pressure, forming a sound wave that you hear as thunder.

What is the speed of light?

186,000 miles per second (300,000 kilometers per second).
All electromagnetic waves travel at the speed of light, from the
longest, the radio waves, through microwaves (for cooking,
transmitting phone calls, and weather radar), infrared (sun's
heat, TV clicker!), visible light, ultraviolet (suntan); X-rays; and
the shortest, interstellar gamma rays.

By comparison, sound travels through air at 344 meters per
second or about 1,130 feet per second (about 760 miles per hour),
give or take, depending on temperature. Mach 1 is the speed of
sound. Sound waves go one mile (1.6 kilometers) in five seconds.

Nautical Measurements

- 1 fathom = 6 feet
- 1 nautical mile = 1.151 statute (land) miles
- 3 nautical miles = 1 league
- 1 knot = 1 nautical mile per hour
- 32 points on a compass equates to 11 1/4 degrees per
  compass point.

If you are standing on a beach, you can see about 2 1/2 to 3 miles
to the horizon, depending on how tall you are.

☐ Other Measurements

☐ A score is 20.

☐ A ream of paper is 500 sheets.

☐ A bale of cotton is 500 pounds.

☐ A chain (in surveying) is 66 feet long (1/10 of a furlong) and is divided into 100 links.

☐ A rod is 16 1/2 feet. 40 rods make a furlong, which is 660 feet.

☐ A fortnight is two weeks.

☐ An acre is 43,560 square feet or 160 square rods.

☐ A pint's a pound the world around. Two pints to a quart, four quarts to a gallon.

☐ A cord of firewood is 128 cubic feet.

☐ Prefixes

There are also steps for tenths (deci) and hundredths (centi). The steps continue after tera with peta (quadrillion), exa (quintillion), zetta (sextillion), and yotta (septillion).

☑ More Science Questions and Answers

☐ How old is the universe?

The universe is estimated at 13.7 billion years old, though scientists are constantly revising this number.

☐ What is a black hole?

A black hole is a dense object in space created by the collapse of a massive star. Because of its immense gravitational pull due to its incredible density, nothing – not even light – can escape a black hole. The area where no escape is possible is the "event horizon." Once inside the event horizon, matter is crushed to a single point of infinite density, known as a "singularity."

We cannot "see" black holes, but scientists find them by locating the swirling gravitational field around them that pulls in anything nearby, including gas, dust, and other space objects like stars and planets. One black hole 50 million light years away was calculated to have a mass equal to three billion of our suns.

☐ What are the planets?

From closest to the Sun to farther from it, the planets in our solar system are:

1. Mercury **2.** Venus **3.** Earth **4.** Mars **5.** Jupiter **6.** Saturn **7.** Uranus **8.** Neptune (**9.** Pluto)

Remember "My Very Excellent Mother Just Served Us Nine Pickles" or "My Very Easy Method. Just Set Up Nine Planets." In 2006, astronomers voted to remove Pluto from the list of planets, re-categorizing it as a "dwarf" planet.

☑ Ages of the Dinosaurs

Triassic = 195 million to 160 million years ago.
Jurassic = 160 million to 125 million years ago.
Cretaceous = 125 million to 60 million years ago.

☑ Geographic Features

Earth's lowest point, the Marianas Trench in the Pacific Ocean, is almost 36,000 feet deep (nearly seven miles or 11,000 meters). The highest point on Earth is Mount Everest, at 29,035 feet (8,850 meters). The longest river is the Nile, at 4,132 miles (6,650 kilometers) long, followed by the Amazon, Yangtze, and Mississippi.

☑ Caves

How to remember which of those things point up and which point down? Stalactites hang "tight" to the roof of the cave so they are the ones that point down. Stalagmites are the ones on the ground that "might" reach up. My wife learned that the "c" in stalactite is for "ceiling," and the "g" in stalagmite is for "ground."

☑ Einstein

What you need to know beyond just $E = mc^2$ and the college dorm poster quoting Einstein's "Great spirits have always found violent opposition from mediocrities."

In 1905 Albert Einstein explained in his Special Theory of Relativity that energy and mass are interchangeable in the famous equation $E = mc^2$, where E = energy, M = mass, and c is the speed of light, squared. The Special Theory also states that the speed of light is the same no matter how observed – nothing travels faster than the speed of light.

Einstein's General Theory of Relativity, published in 1916, demonstrated that space and time are connected and that space time can be distorted by matter and energy. In Einstein's theory, there is no absolute space or time. The General Theory predicts black holes, posits that gravity bends light, and helps explain the Big Bang.

MATH NOTE: Pi or π = 3.14159 and so on. It is the ratio of the circumference of a circle to its diameter. What that means is to find the circumference of a circle multiply the diameter by Pi ($C = \pi \times D$). To find the area, multiply Pi by the radius squared ($A = \pi \times r^2$).

☑ Metal and Alloys

For some reason men like metals (or maybe that's just me). Anyway, not that it comes up that often, but sometimes it's interesting to know what metals make up certain alloys.

☐ Brass = Copper and Zinc. Used for brass rings, musical instruments, brass beds, candlesticks, shell casings, brass knuckles, and plumbing fittings.

☐ Bronze = Copper and Tin. Used in sculpture, preserving baby shoes, bells, third place medals, plumbing fittings, and (with manganese) boat propellers.

☐ Pewter = mostly tin with some copper and antimony. Pewter used to be made of tin and lead.

☐ Steel = Iron minus most of its carbon (down to 0.5–1.5%

carbon). Stainless steel contains 10–30% chromium and usually some nickel. Steel may also contain cobalt, molybdenum, manganese, vanadium, or tungsten, depending on what it's going to be used for. Steel is smelted from iron ore and coal (coke, or purified coal) with limestone also used to remove impurities, with other elements such as chromium added as needed.

☑ Metal as Money

A standard gold bar weighs 27 1/2 pounds (400 ounces). At $1,600 an ounce, it would be worth $640,000. Since 1982 pennies have been manufactured with copper plating (2.5%) around a zinc core (97.5%). Before that, pennies were 95% copper/5% zinc.

A digression on coins: Each coin has two mottos on it, "In God We Trust" and "E Pluribus Unum" ("Out of many, one," referring to the formation of the United States). A penny weighs 2.5 grams, a nickel 5 grams. A penny is 3/4 inches in diameter (1.55 millimeters thick), a quarter nearly an inch in diameter (0.955 inch). Coins weigh the same on each side. Statistically a coin has a 50% chance of landing on the side you call. Quarters, dimes, and half dollars have copper cores and an outer cladding of 75/25 copper/copper-nickel alloy, the same material that nickels are made of.

And I've always been curious how metal detectors worked. So I looked into it. They operate using electromagnetism. The detector part that you see beachcombers waving over the sand has metal with electricity flowing through it. When the detector passes over a metal object, the object disrupts or distorts the electromagnetic field. When that happens it triggers the warning noise to signal buried treasure.

☑ Chemicals

☐ Sodium chloride (chemical symbol NaCl) is table salt.

☐ Silicon dioxide (SiO_2) is sand. Glass is made from sand, soda ash, and lime (calcium carbonate).

☐ Air we breathe is about 78% nitrogen (N), 21% oxygen (O), and the rest other gases (like argon (Ar) and neon (Ne)) along with carbon dioxide (CO_2) and water vapor (H_2O). Ozone is oxygen in a different form, three atoms (O_3) instead of the usual two together (O_2).

☐ H_2O is water (two hydrogen atoms, one oxygen atom).

☐ Calcium carbonate ($CaCO_3$) is chalk, marble, or limestone. It is also used for antacids.

☐ Club soda contains carbon dioxide gas (CO_2) to make it fizz.

☐ Diamonds are made up of carbon atoms. Petroleum products (gasoline, natural gas, kerosene) are hydrocarbons, carbon atoms with varying numbers of hydrogen atoms.

"When I was a boy of 14, my father was so ignorant I could hardly stand to have the old man around. But when I got to be 21, I was astonished at how much he learned in seven years."
—*Mark Twain*

☐ Gunpowder is made from charcoal (C), potassium nitrate (KNO_3 or saltpeter), and sulfur (S).

Contrails or condensation trails left by jets are formed by condensation of water vapor that is a byproduct of burning jet fuel.

Acids and bases are measured on the pH scale, ranging from 0 to 14, with pure water at 7. Other values: 0 hydrochloric acid, 2 lemon juice, 5 coffee and beer, 8 seawater and blood, 9 soap, 11 ammonia, and 14 drain cleaner.

The periodic table contains 91 natural elements. Of those 91 elements, 11 are gases (like oxygen, nitrogen, and neon) and two are liquids (mercury and bromine). The rest are solid at room temperature. Polymers are long chains of naturally-occurring molecules as with our DNA and carbohydrates in our food, or man-made molecules (often with a petroleum base), as with nylon and Teflon.

☑ Newton's Laws

1. A body in motion tends to remain in motion.
2. Force equals mass times acceleration.
3. For every action there is an equal and opposite reaction.

The First Law applies to spaceships and children. The Second Law is known by the famous equation $F = M \times A$. The Third Law does not apply when you tell your children it is bedtime as the reaction will be unequal.

☑ The Six Types of Machines

1. Inclined Plane
2. Lever
3. Wedge
4. Wheel
5. Pulley
6. Screw

☑ Science Tricks

☐ The Indestructible Balloon

You can poke it with a pin or burn it, and this indestructible balloon will still not burst. You can first have fun by taking two regular blown up balloons. With the first, poke it with a pin. BLAMM! Take the second, and hold a match up to it. BLAMM! Now, do the following:

Cross pieces of wide adhesive tape in an **X** shape on an inflated balloon. Now you can push a pin through the middle of the **X**, where the pieces of tape cross. Nothing happens! The tape (usually) holds the balloon together so it does not explode.

You can also hold a match up to a balloon, and it will not burst. Put some water in a balloon and then inflate it the rest of the way. Now, wave a match under the balloon, right where the water is. Even when the flame touches the balloon, it does not explode. The flame from the match is heating the water; the water is absorbing enough heat that the balloon does not burst.

☐ Under Pressure

This experiment with underwater divers shows the effects of air pressure. Fill a one or two liter plastic soft drink bottle to the very top with water.

Prepare to dive! Make a "diver." You can use a disposable pen cap (make sure the top part does not have holes). Weight down the bottom (open end). You could wrap some wire around the bottom or attach a paper clip or two. The weight should be just enough to keep the diver upright in the water without sinking. Put the diver in the water, which should be to the very top. Make sure that there is some air in the diver when you place it in the ocean. Screw on the bottle top.

Diver away! Squeeze the bottle. Your diver should sink.
How this works. The air in the diver is compressed when you squeeze the sides of the bottle. (The one liter bottle I used was kind of hard to squeeze.) Water is forced into the "diver," the only place it can go. The added water makes the diver sink. Submarines work this way by taking on water or forcing it out to increase buoyancy. When you release the sides of the bottle, the pressure on the diver is released, the air in the diver pushes the extra water out, and the diver floats up.

☐ Bubble Power

Fill a glass with club soda. Drop in a few raisins.
Watch 'em dance.

How this works. The bubbles gather on the raisins, giving them enough lift to let them float up. When the bubbles escape, the raisin sinks until it accumulates new bubbles.

☐ Soap Boat

Take an index card or piece of cardboard and cut it down to 2½ inches by 1½ inches. Make one end pointed, like the bow of a boat. On the other side, the back of the boat, cut a square notch in the middle about ¾ inch wide and ½ inches deep.

Gently set the boat in some water. Pour a few drops of liquid detergent in the notch area at the back of the boat. The boat will sail across the ocean. The soap breaks the surface tension of the water enough to force the boat ahead.

Our Science
Experiments

☐ _____

☐ _____

☐ _____

☐ _____

☐ _____

☐ Alka Seltzer Rocket

This is a low power "starter" rocket. Fill a 35 mm film canister about 1/3 with water. Drop an Alka-Seltzer in the canister. Put the top on. Turn the canister upside down. Stand back for launch!

☐ Bag Bomb

In a ziploc bag, put ½ cup water and ½ cup vinegar. Place 2 teaspoons baking soda in a quarter sheet of paper towel and fold it up. Drop the baking soda packet into the ziploc bag and quickly zip shut. Shake and stand back for the pop. Yeah!

☐ Light and Water Optics

Take a small glass jar like for mustard, punch two small holes in the metal top. Tape a flashlight to the bottom of the jar (duct tape – a dad's friend). Then tape all around the rest of the glass so it is covered. Fill the jar with water and screw the top on. Turn on the flashlight. Pour water out of the lower hole. You should see it lit up.

☑ More Science and References

Five important inventions and discoveries:

☐ Printing Press
☐ Electricity
☐ Steam Engine and Railroad
☐ Television
☐ Internet

☐ International Morse Code

- A dash is equal to three dots.
- The space between parts of the same letter is equal to one dot.
- The space between two letters is equal to three dots.
- The space between two words is equal to seven dots.

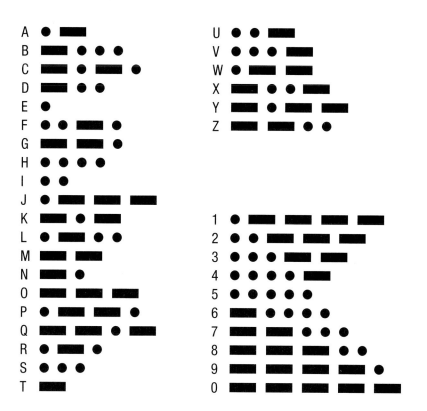

☐ The Greek Alphabet

A	B	Γ	Δ	E
Alpha	**Beta**	**Gamma**	**Delta**	**Epsilon**
Z	H	Θ	I	K
Zeta	**Eta**	**Theta**	**Iota**	**Kappa**
Λ	M	N	Ξ	O
Lambda	**Mu**	**Nu**	**Xi**	**Omicron**
Π	P	Σ	T	Υ
Pi	**Rho**	**Sigma**	**Tau**	**Upsilon**
Φ	X	Ψ	Ω	
Phi	**Chi**	**Psi**	**Omega**	

☐ Quick Conversions Reference

From	To	Conversion (rounded)
Inches	Centimeters	Multiply by 2.54
Feet	Meters	Multiply by 0.3
Miles	Kilometers	Multiply by 1.61
Gallons	Liters	Multiply by 3.8
Ounces	Grams	Multiply by 28.35
Pounds	Kilograms	Multiply by 0.45
Centimeters	Inches	Multiply by 0.39
Meters	Feet	Multiply by 3.28
Kilometers	Miles	Multiply by 0.62
Liters	Gallons	Multiply by 0.26
Grams	Ounces	Multiply by 0.035
Kilograms	Pounds	Multiply by 2.2

Freezing point: 32 degrees F = 0 degrees C
Boiling point: 212 degrees F = 100 degrees C

A simple rule of thumb to convert Celsius to Fahrenheit: Double C and add 32. It gets you close to the actual temperature. The other way, F to C, subtract 32 and divide in half. Again, you will get pretty close to the actual number.

The Culture Checklist

A sweet thing, for whatever time, to revisit in dreams the dear dad we have lost.

– Euripides

Sports, Outdoors, Cars – those are pretty typical dad topics. But dads are Renaissance men, ready to recite *The Road Not Taken*, willing to dress in a sharp tuxedo for a big night out, and able to sing Little Bunny Foo Foo when the occasion demands.

 # Word Play

☐ Three Great Poems for Children

Where Go the Boats?
  – Robert Louis Stevenson

Dark brown is the river,
Golden is the sand.
It flows along for ever,
With trees on either hand.
Green leaves a-floating,
Castles of the foam,
Boats of mine a-boating--
Where will all come home?

On goes the river
And out past the mill,
Away down the valley,
Away down the hill.

Away down the river,
A hundred miles or more,
Other little children
Shall bring my boats ashore.

Fog
– Carl Sandburg

The fog comes on little cat feet.
It sits looking over harbor and city
on silent haunches and then moves on.

The Road Not Taken
– Robert Frost

Two roads diverged in a yellow wood,
And sorry I could not travel both
And be one traveler, long I stood
And looked down one as far as I could
To where it bent in the undergrowth;
Then took the other, as just as fair,
And having perhaps the better claim,
Because it was grassy and wanted wear;
Though as for that the passing there
Had worn them really about the same,
And both that morning equally lay
In leaves no step had trodden black.
Oh, I kept the first for another day!
Yet knowing how way leads on to way,
I doubted if I should ever come back.
I shall be telling this with a sigh
Somewhere ages and ages hence:
Two roads diverged in a wood, and I —
I took the one less traveled by,
And that has made all the difference.

> **CULTURE NOTE:** Old terms that have different meanings than when they originated: dial a phone, cut and paste, clicker for remote control, broken record, "cc" for carbon copy, clockwise, ticker tape parade, telegraph your intentions.

☐ And One for Parents

Our Favorite Poems

☐ _____

_____

☐ _____

_____

☐ _____

_____

☐ _____

_____

Musée des Beaux Arts

– W.H. Auden

About suffering they were never wrong,
The Old Masters: how well they understood
Its human position; how it takes place
While someone else is eating or opening a window or just
      walking dully along;
How when the aged are reverently, passionately waiting
For the miraculous birth, there always must be
Children who did not specially want it to happen, skating
On a pond at the edge of the wood:
They never forgot
That even the dreadful martyrdom must run its course
Anyhow in a corner, some untidy spot
Where the dogs go on with their doggy life and the torturer's horse
Scratches its innocent behind on a tree.
In Brueghel's Icarus, for instance: how everything turns away
Quite leisurely from the disaster; the ploughman may
Have heard the splash, the forsaken cry,
But for him it was not an important failure; the sun shone
As it had to on the white legs disappearing into the green
Water; and the expensive delicate ship that must have seen
Something amazing, a boy falling out of the sky,
Had somewhere to get to and sailed calmly on.

☐ Onyms

Acronym: Word made of first letters of words of phrase like SCUBA for self-contained underwater breathing apparatus and LASER for light amplification by the stimulated emission of radiation.

Aptronym or Euonym: Where a person's name fits his profession like poet Wordsworth, law professor Judge, optometrist Seymour, and White House spokesman Speakes.

Eponym: Name that has come to mean the thing like Earl of Sandwich for a sandwich, Romulus for Rome, braille for Louis Braille, a John Hancock, and Machiavellian.

Homonym: Words that sound alike but have different meanings like raise and raze, doe and dough, dear and deer, and pear and pair and pare.

☐ Fun Oxymorons

- Airline schedule
- Jumbo shrimp
- Random order
- Small crowd
- Pretty ugly
- Big sip
- Tech support
- Computer security
- Home office
- Industrial park
- Working vacation

☐ Language Fun

Palindromes read the same forward and backward: kayak, civic, radar, racecar. Madam, I'm Adam. A man, a plan, a canal, Panama! I prefer Pi. A Santa at NASA. Never odd or even.

☐ Three Songs for Young Children

Head, Shoulders, Knees and Toes
(done with lots of pointing)

Head, shoulders, knees and toes, knees and toes.
Head, shoulders, knees and toes, knees and toes.
Eyes and ears and mouth and nose.
Head, shoulders, knees and toes, knees and toes.

Little Birds
(using appropriate arm gestures)

Waaaayyyy up in the sky, The little birds fly,
While down in the nest, The little birds rest.

With a wing on the left, And a wing on the right,
The little birds slumber, All through the night.

SHHHH! You'll wake the darn birds!

The bright sun comes up, The dew falls away,
"Good morning, good morning!" The little birds say.

Little Bunny Foo Foo

Little bunny foo-foo hoppin' through the forest,
Scoopin' up the field mice,
And boppin' 'em on the head.

Along came the good fairy, and she said:
"Little bunny foo-foo, I don't want to see you,
Scoopin' up the field mice,
And boppin' 'em on the head.
I'll give you three chances, and if you don't obey,
I'll turn you into a goon."

So the next day, [Repeat with two more chances]
So the next day, [Repeat with one more chance]
So the next day, [Repeat]

"I gave you three chances to change and you didn't
obey, so now I'm going to turn you into a goon.
Poof. You're a goon."

(And the moral of the story is "Hare today, goon tomorrow!")

Our Favorite
Songs and Rhymes

☐ _____

☐ _____

☐ _____

☐ _____

☐ _____

☐ **("Just one more") An Added Bedtime Song**

Taps

Day is done, gone the sun,
From the lakes, from the hills, from the sky;
All is well, safely rest, God is nigh.

✔ Cultural Stuff

☐ Clothing

Earlier, I talked about how to change a tire, Here, I talk about how to change attire.

Tux. The cummerbund around your waist should have the pleats (I didn't want to use that word but couldn't think of anything else) facing up. That is to "catch crumbs" or "hold your tickets," in theory, but I wouldn't count on it. If your tux shirt has a pointed collar, the points go down. You don't have to learn how to tie a bowtie; you can use the pre-tied ones if you want.

Ties. For regular ties, there are three basic ways to knot it, but most of us tie the "Four-In-Hand" and not the Windsor or Half-Windsor.

> **Step 1.** Loop your tie with the wide end on the right side. The thin end should reach down to about the last button on your shirt (experiment to find the right spot for you). Take the wide end in your right hand, pass it over the top of the thin end hanging down, and loop around behind the thin end and up through to come back down on the left.
>
> **Step 2.** Pass the wide end all the way around the back across the front and then push the wide end up through the back of the loop.
>
> **Step 3.** Bring the wide end back down through the loop in front.
>
> **Step 4.** Pull tight, up to the collar while sliding the knot up. Center, flip down collar if you have not already, and make sure that you button the collar down if it has buttons.

☐ Some Famous Groupings

Pairs. Laurel and Hardy, Batman and Robin, Adam and Eve, Jack and Jill, Dick and Jane, Lone Ranger and Tonto, Romeo and Juliet, Rocky and Bullwinkle, salt and pepper, apples and oranges, Scylla and Charybdis, Tom and Huck.

Trios. The Three Patriarchs Abraham, Isaac, and Jacob; Three Fates: (Clotho spins the thread, Lachesis decides the length, and Atropos cuts the thread); Three Stooges; Tinkers to Evers to Chance; Kingston Trio; Charlie's Angels; Snap, Crackle, and Pop; Three Wise Men; Faith, Hope, and Charity; The Good, the Bad, and the Ugly; the Three Musketeers.

Quartets. Four Horsemen of the Apocalypse (Conquest or Slaughter, War, Famine, Death), Four Horsemen of Notre Dame, Fab Four (the Beatles).

Fives. Ancient Olympia Pentathlon (race, discus, javelin, long jump, wrestling), classical architectural orders (Doric, Ionic, Corinthian, Composite, Tuscan).

Sevens. Seven Wonders: the Great Pyramids, the Hanging Gardens of Babylon, Statue of Zeus at Olympia, Temple of Artemis at Ephesus, Mausoleum of Halicarnassus, Colussus at Rhodes, the Lighthouse (Pharos) of Alexandria; Seven Deadly Sins: pride, envy, sloth, wrath, avarice, gluttony, lust; Seven Hills of Rome; Seven Liberal Arts of the Medieval Curriculum: grammar, rhetoric, logic, arithmetic, geometry, music, astronomy.

Nines. Nine Muses: Calliope (epic poetry), Clio (history), Erato (lyric or love poetry), Euterpe (music), Melpomene (tragedy), Polyhymnia (sacred poetry), Terpsichore (dance), Thalia (comedy), Urania (astronomy).

Tens. Decathlon (100 meter sprint, long jump, shot put, high jump, 400 meter race, 110-meter hurdles, discus, pole vault, javelin, 1500 meter race).

Twelves. Greek Gods, Tribes of Israel, Knights of the Roundtable.

Our Favorite Books

☐ _____

☐ _____

☐ _____

☐ _____

☐ _____

☐ Top 10 Fiction Books (from Modern Library)

1. *Ulysses,* James Joyce
2. *The Great Gatsby,* F. Scott Fitzgerald
3. *A Portrait of the Artist as a Young Man,* James Joyce
4. *Lolita,* Vladimir Nabokov
5. *Brave New World,* Aldous Huxley
6. *The Sound and the Fury,* William Faulkner
7. *Catch-22,* Joseph Heller
8. *Darkness at Noon,* Arthur Koestler
9. *Sons and Lovers,* D.H. Lawrence
10. *The Grapes of Wrath,* John Steinbeck

☐ Top 10 Movies for All Time
(According to the American Film Institute)

1. *Citizen Kane* (1941)
2. *Casablanca* (1942)
3. *The Godfather* (1972)
4. *Gone with the Wind* (1939)
5. *Lawrence of Arabia* (1962)
6. *The Wizard of Oz* (1939)
7. *The Graduate* (1967)
8. *On the Waterfront* (1954)
9. *Schindler's List* (1993)
10. *Singin' in the Rain* (1952)

☐ Poems

Poetry can be inspiring, thought-provoking, and understandable. Try "Poetry 180: A Poem a Day for American High Schools."

Our Favorite Movies

☐ _____

☐ _____

☐ _____

☐ _____

☐ _____

United States Presidents and Terms of Office

President	Office Term	President	Office Term
George Washington	1789–1797	Benjamin Harrison	1889–1893
John Adams	1797–1801	Grover Cleveland	1893–1897
Thomas Jefferson	1801–1809	William McKinley	1897–1901
James Madison	1809–1817	Theodore Roosevelt	1901–1909
James Monroe	1817–1825	William Howard Taft	1909–1913
John Quincy Adams	1825–1829	Woodrow Wilson	1913–1921
Andrew Jackson	1829–1837	Warren G. Harding	1921–1923
Martin Van Buren	1837–1841	Calvin Coolidge	1923–1929
William Henry Harrison	1841	Herbert Hoover	1929–1933
John Tyler	1841–1845	Franklin D. Roosevelt	1933–1945
James K. Polk	1845–1849	Harry S Truman	1945–1953
Zachary Taylor	1849–1850	Dwight D. Eisenhower	1953–1961
Millard Fillmore	1850–1853	John F. Kennedy	1961–1963
Franklin Pierce	1853–1857	Lyndon B. Johnson	1963–1969
James Buchanan	1857–1861	Richard Nixon	1969–1974
Abraham Lincoln	1861–1865	Gerald Ford	1974–1977
Andrew Johnson	1865–1869	Jimmy Carter	1977–1981
Ulysses S. Grant	1869–1877	Ronald Reagan	1981–1989
Rutherford B. Hayes	1877–1881	George H.W. Bush	1989–1993
James A. Garfield	1881	William J. Clinton	1993–2001
Chester A. Arthur	1881–1885	George W. Bush	2001– 2009
Grover Cleveland	1885–1889	Barack Obama	2009–Present

The Fun Checklist

Dads are leaders in fun: fun trips, folding paper airplanes, card games, and some easy tricks.

Short Trips

☐ Walk in the park with a picnic lunch and a ball to kick or throw

☐ Trip to science museum and lunch at cafeteria

☐ Jaunt to art museum and lunch at cafe

☐ Walk in the woods near your home

☐ Trip to the beach, river, or lake no matter what the weather or season

☐ Apple picking

☐ Watch planes at the airport

☐ Take a short train ride

☐ Explore around the neighborhood

✓ Tricks and Puzzles

☐ Card Trick

This is an easy one for your child to learn. Take a deck of cards. Glance at the bottom card. This is the key card. Have your child pick a card from the deck and remember it. Then, he should put the card back on the top of the deck. Cut the cards, placing the bottom half of the deck on top of the card on top. You can have your child cut the cards too now that you have set up the deck. The card your child selected is the one after the key card.

☐ Tangram

Tangrams let you create thousands of shapes by arranging the cut out pieces. You can create a dog, bear, fish, horse, bird, and rabbit. Tangrams can be bought or made from tracing the diagram below on a larger piece of paper and cutting it out, or using the method to the right.

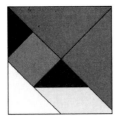
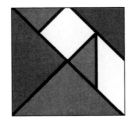

1.

Fold a rectangular piece of paper to form a square. Cut off the extra flap.

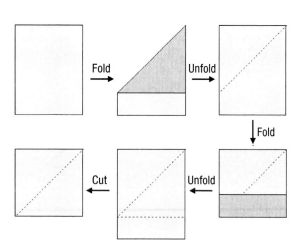

2.

Cut the large square into two equal triangles.

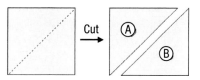

3.

Take one triangle and fold it in half. Cut that triangle along the fold into two smaller triangles.

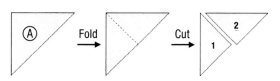

4.

Take the other large
triangle and crease it in
the middle. Fold the corner
of the triangle opposite
the crease and cut.

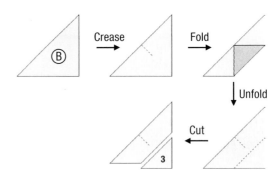

5.

Fold the remaining
trapezoid in half and
fold again. Cut along
both folds.

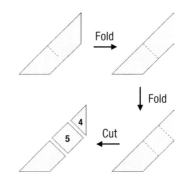

6.

Fold the remaining small
trapezoid and cut it in two.

There you have it, the tangram pieces. Some examples below:

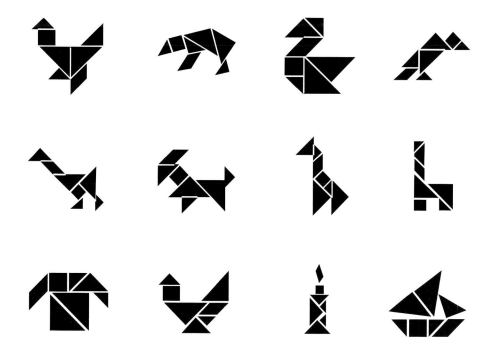

☑ Guess a Color

1. Write the names of the following colors on index cards or pieces of paper: Red, Blue, Green, Yellow, Magenta, and Lavender. Each color has a different number of letters, from three to eight.

2. Spread the cards face up on a table. Mix them around. Then lay them out in some order.

3. Have your child select a color without telling you which one she picked.

4. Ask her to spell the color in her head as you point to the cards.

5. Each time you point to a card, your child should think of the next letter in the color.

6. Tell her to say "Stop" when she finishes spelling the color.

7. Point to any card at first, and any card for the second one.

8. For the third card, point to red, blue for the fourth, green for the fifth, etc. until she finishes spelling. When she says "Stop" you will be pointing at her color.

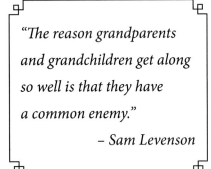

"The reason grandparents and grandchildren get along so well is that they have a common enemy."
— Sam Levenson

☑ Write in Invisible Ink

Use a toothpick to write with lemon juice on a piece of paper. Let dry. It will be invisible. To see the secret message, hold the paper carefully near a hot lightbulb. As the paper heats up, the secret message will appear.

☑ Mnemonics

☐ ROY G BIV: Colors of the rainbow—Red, Orange, Yellow, Green, Blue, Indigo, Violet.

☐ "I" before "e" except after "c" or in rhyming with A as in neighbor or weigh.

☐ HOMES: The Great Lakes – Huron Ontario Michigan Erie Superior.

☐ EGBDF: Lines on the musical scale – Every Good Boy Deserves Fun.

☐ FACE: Spaces on the musical scale.

☐ 30 days hath September, April, June and November. All the rest have 31, except February which has 28 (29 in leap year).

Another way to remember how many days are in a month is to hold out your left hand in a fist (this method is easy to use, hard to explain in words). The knuckle on the farthest left is January, with 31 days. Next is the gap in between the first two knuckles, which is February (28). Next knuckle is March, again with 31. Gap in between the second and third knuckles is April, with 30 days.

The pattern is each knuckle is a month with 31 days, each space a month with 30 days (except February). The way to do it is to count across, and you end at July on the fourth knuckle (you don't use the thumb knuckle or space before it). Then you go back with August, staying on that fourth knuckle (or going on to fist of right hand).

☑ Paper Folding (Origami)

☐ Basic Office Paper Airplane

1. Take a sheet of paper and fold it in half lengthwise.

2. Open it up, and fold the two top corners down to the middle crease.

3. Fold entire sheet in half lengthwise, so now you have a pointed piece or nose of the plane.

4. On each half, fold down part of the paper to form wings (a quarter sheet). Push up so the wings are perpendicular to the fuselage.

5. To make the plane fly better, attach a paperclip to the nose. This gives the plane some weight and better balance.

Variation on a Paper Airplane – The Hoop Plane

Cut a 3x5 file card into three equal strips the long way (so you have three 1x5 strips). Take one of the strips and tape the ends together to form a small circle. Take the other two strips, tape the ends together, and then tape the other free ends together to form a large circle.

Tape the large circle to the back of a straw. Tape the small circle to the front of the straw, so that it lines up with the larger circle in back. Hold the straw part, and throw. Like the basic paper airplane, try a paperclip in the front.

Variation on a Paper Airplane – The Supersonic Jet

There are lots and lots of paper airplane designs. This one seems to work well, and it's a fun design to experiment with.

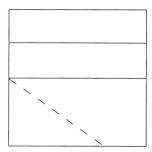

1. Fold a square sheet of paper in half, and then fold one half again so that you have a quarter and a half mark. Then, fold the bottom left corner up to meet the middle mark.

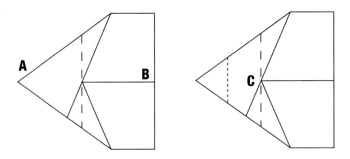

2. Then fold the top left corner to the middle mark along the line shown. Fold the tip **A** to the middle of the base, **B**, then open up to show the crease. Now, fold the tip A to the crease you just made, at **C**.

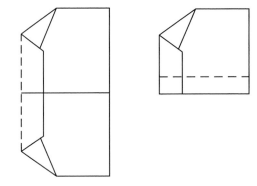

3. Fold in half. Fold wings down along dotted line. The blunt-nosed supersonic jet is ready to fly.

☑ The Best Origami – The Popper

Although there are so many things you can make by folding paper (hats, boats, planes, boxes), the best is this popper since it makes a lot of noise.

1. Take a full sheet of newspaper. Hold the folded edge at the top, open edges at bottom.

2. Fold the top down in half, then open so that you have a crease in the middle.

3. Fold the four corners to the crease.

4. Fold the entire paper in half, lengthwise.

5. Fold in half along the width.

6. You will have two points at the top. Take one point and fold it down on its side, and then take the other point and fold down on the opposite side.

7. Hold the points you just folded down and flick your wrist to "pop" the popper.

 # Poker

The best to worst hands:

Royal Flush =
Five highest cards, 10
through Ace, same suit.

Straight Flush =
Five cards of the same
suit in order.

Four of a Kind

Full House =
Three of the same cards
and a pair.

Flush =
Five cards of same suit.

Straight =
Five cards in order.

Three of a Kind

Two Pair

Pair

High Card

There are many variations of poker. Texas Hold 'Em has become popular, but five card draw is a good game. In Texas Hold 'Em, the small blind bets first, half the minimum bet. The big blind bets next, with the minimum bet, both before the cards are dealt. Then, the dealer deals two pocket cards face down to each player. The next person calls, raises, or folds. Betting goes around the table. The last one before the first person who bet is the button (who is the dealer in a game with friends). After the first round of betting, the dealer turns over three cards, the flop, and there is another round of betting. Next, the turn card is shown; more betting. Finally, the river card is turned over; more betting. Best hand left wins the pot.

☐ Hearts

Played with four people, the goal of hearts is usually to have the least number of points by avoiding getting any heart suit cards (worth one point each) and the Queen of Spades (worth 13 points).

Deal out the entire deck, 13 cards each. Take three cards you want to discard from your hand. In the first round, you pass left. You will later pass right, then across, then keep. Two of clubs leads. You must play the suit led if you have it. If not, you can play any suit, including hearts.

If you have the high card (aces are high), you win the trick and lead the next one. You can lead with any suit except hearts unless a heart has been played (because someone did not have that suit) or you have no other suit.

Play goes around from the left of the lead. Winner of the trick then leads. Play until all cards have been played. Count up the score. Usually you play until someone reaches 100 points. Low score wins.

You can "shoot the moon" by trying to take all the hearts and the queen of spades. If you are successful, you get zero points and all other players receive 26 points. If you are only partially successful, you have a handful of hearts and queen of spades – a lot of points.

The Family *Checklist*

We cannot always build the future for our youth, but we can build our youth for the future.

– Franklin Delano Roosevelt

There is no 100% complete, one-size-fits-all Dad checklist for being a family. The ideas below are small steps to building the relationship with your children and passing along not lessons, exactly, but more like examples that will help them grow.

☑ Small Steps

☐ #1 is spend time with your child doing things he or she wants to do. But just spend time with them. This means routine activities and daily stuff like cooking and sitting down to a meal or helping clean up toys or reading to them before bed. (TV time does not count as time together, unless it falls under the "Red Sox [Insert your team here] could win it this year if they win this game and we have to be here to give them good luck" exception.) Along with #1 is spending time with your wife.

☐ Even when the last thing you want to do is what you're being asked to do and you're exhausted and have a million other things to do, remember the request is the number one most important thing in the world that your child wants to do. Also, your child likes to do things that occasionally are not so great – too much candy, too much screen time – but also occasionally it's ok to indulge them so long as it's not too often. Sometimes we snack too much or watch too much TV also.

☐ Set limits. Provide discipline, and show control. Be consistent and firm, but reasonable. Make the discipline equal the transgression and have it connected and proportional. Let them apologize and occasionally have ways to reduce the penalty. Yes, be firm, but also show flexibility.

☐ And say "yes." Yes, we can play baseball when you finish cleaning your room. Yes, you can have a cookie once you finish your apple. Yes, I would like to build blocks with you, once I finish the dishes.

> **FAMILY NOTE:**
> Remember with children: Good judgment comes from experience; experience comes from bad judgment.

☐ Think about what it's like to be under four feet tall and less than 50 pounds and everyone tells you what to do. Get down eye to eye to talk sometimes. This will give both of you a new angle on a problem.

☐ Listen carefully to what your child is saying and how he or she is saying it. Don't interrupt. Don't belittle or dismiss what they are saying. Don't say it is silly. You're the grown up and don't have to respond with emotion (easier said than done). Give your child a way to make amends.

☐ Hold hands, hug.

☐ Teach your child to break a challenge into pieces, to meet a problem one step at a time. This works for homework and for climbing a mountain.

Our Family Tree

☐ Read to your child – a lot.

☑ Create a Family Tree

We look to the future, but we learn from the past. Create a family tree. Include stories about what your mother and father did, where they lived, where they came from, how they got here. Go back as far as you can. If your parents are still around, ask them to think about their parents and grandparents and to tell stories about growing up, the good and the bad. Then go out and plant a real tree for each child.

Recall the story President Kennedy told about French Marshal Lyautey, who asked his gardener to plant a tree. The gardener objected that the tree was slow-growing and would not reach maturity for a 100 years. The Marshal replied, "In that case, there is no time to lose. Plant it this afternoon."

FAMILY NOTE:
One of my favorite sayings: It's not the size of the dog in the fight, it's the size of the fight in the dog.

☑ More Small Steps

☐ Tell bedtime stories.

☐ Teach honor, respect and self-respect, civility, history, and religion.

☐ Treat Mom to flowers, kids to ice cream.

☐ Teach them about practice and hard work.

☐ Praise them when they earn it, but don't overpraise. Focus on the effort. Catch them doing something right. Look for opportunities to tell them they are doing the right thing or to thank them.

☐ It is ok to be wrong and to apologize to your children. You do not have to be infallible. You do not have to "win" every time.

☐ If they are wrong, correct them. But not in anger (if you can help it), and not in front of others (if you can avoid it). Not all mistakes are equal, either, so discipline should be proportionate.

☐ Adversity doesn't build character. It reveals it. So help them build character, by letting them deal with the consequences of their actions.

☐ Most of all, show them that you love them.

☑ A Concluding Poem

Those Winter Sundays

– Robert Hayden

Sundays too my father got up early
and put his clothes on in the blueblack cold,
then with cracked hands that ached
from labor in the weekday weather made
banked fires blaze. No one ever thanked him.

I'd wake and hear the cold splintering, breaking.
When the rooms were warm, he'd call,
and slowly I would rise and dress,
fearing the chronic angers of that house,
speaking indifferently to him,
who had driven out the cold
and polished my good shoes as well.
What did I know, what did I know
of love's austere and lonely offices?

✓ A Final Thought

Be kind, for everyone you meet is fighting a hard battle.

—Plato

About the Author

Raised in Memphis, Jeff Levinson has led canoeing and hiking trips, built furniture, worked on two presidential campaigns, bartended, played sports, coached kids' soccer, done volunteer work, earned graduate degrees, and advised companies in fields of technology, publishing, business skills, and construction procurement. None of that prepared him for being a Dad. Jeff now lives in Boston with his wife and two sons.